DEAR SON

Letters and reflections from First Nations fathers and sons

THOMAS MAYO

Aboriginal and Torres Strait Islander readers are warned that this book includes the names and images of people who have died.

DEAR SON

Letters and reflections from First Nations fathers and sons

THOMAS MAYO

Design and illustrations by Tristan Schultz
Artwork by Tony Wilson

Hardie Grant
EXPLORE

Dear First Nations men,

Together we will unlearn what we were taught in the coloniser's missions, slave camps, prisons, ghettos, and in the Australian media. We will sing our culture, healing the earth, as our grandfathers did for more than sixty millennia. We will love ourselves and our families, and we will return to our rightful place in Australia.

We will celebrate who we are,
as we have always deserved to do.

In unity,

Thomas Mayo

Foreword

There is no shame job here. These letters, written to both sons and fathers of sons, are delicate, raw, honest, and always loving.

I'm not surprised by the tenderness on these pages, as I myself grew up with a Wiradjuri, Gundungurra, Ngunawal father who was hard and soft, whole and broken, but above all – *loving.* I'm the daughter, the woman and the mother I am today because of the father I had.

There is such a great responsibility to *be* a father, to step up to that role to guide one's children, to be a pillar of strength in the family and community, at home and work. Sometimes the expectation and pressure to appear strong, coupled with the trauma many of our men carry, has led to difficulties with family or with the law.

These stories don't shy away from introspection on those issues. Yet within these pages are the words of sculptors. What I mean is that these men have taken the clay material of the past – all that trauma of colonial weight – and with it, all that water of community – thousands and thousands of years of culture, family, Country – and have made something else. These men have chosen to sculpt – and there is the beauty of each of these letters. They have shared with the young men and boys of today and tomorrow the lessons they have learnt. They have shown them how to make something solid out of all the materials we've been bestowed with. In the end and along the way, that is what matters.

The demonisation of the Blak man is a colonial stain. Psychologically and emotionally harmful at best, detrimental and life threatening at its worst. When Thomas and I met, I knew he was a great role model. I think we spoke about this book so early in our talking because we were both concerned by the lies and stereotypes about First Nations men being thrown around in the media at the time, and since we were kids ourselves.

This book is about dispelling the stereotype around what masculinity is for First Nations men. Being open, talking up, yarning – about sexuality, about running amok, gender roles, the white heteronormative patriarchy in Australia, drugs and alcohol, mental health, love, careers, family, and the weight of both trauma and culture. This book addresses strong cultural ties and also the shame that has historically pervaded those who have been affected by the loss of culture, family and language through the impact of colonialism. It's all here. Also, in these letters, there is great evidence of our men's contributions to our nation.

First Nations men have made a huge contribution to the progress of Australia as we know it today, as workers, veterans, politicians, artists, and activists since colonisation. This book is also a celebration, acknowledgement and affirmation of that effort and survival.

Here also are conversations with women, because our feminism is part of men's business too. These letters pay homage to our mothers and sisters, starting a real conversation that is necessary for our future power.

This book is a call to readers to take up the pen for their own sons and fathers, daughters and mothers. To write a letter about all those unsaid things, and to act – knowing that affection, truthfulness and softness are not only representative of maternal love, but paternal love too.

In solidarity,

Tara June Winch

Tara June Winch is a Wiradjuri essayist and author of Swallow the Air, After the Carnage *and* The Yield. *She is the recipient of the Miles Franklin Award and Prime Minister's Literary Award, among others.*

Contents

CELEBRATING FIRST NATIONS MEN – AN ACT OF DEFIANCE

When First Nations men love ourselves we are better able to love our families and communities. Yet loving ourselves is an act of defiance.

Since the beginning of the European invasion of our homes on the Australian continent and adjacent islands, colonial institutions have been teaching my people to hate who we are.

As a boy in school, I was taught that my forefathers were unintelligent and inhuman, while my white friends were taught that their forefathers were great explorers, builders, inventors, and our saviours.

Later, as a young man and the father of three Aboriginal and Torres Strait Islander babies, I saw the *Racial Discrimination Act 1975* suspended by Prime Minister John Howard, putting Blak families like mine in peril. With blatant discrimination made legal once again, Howard imposed the 2007 Northern Territory National Emergency Response, or as others called it, The Intervention. As part of The Intervention's measures, Aboriginal community leaders were disempowered, with all manner of hard-fought-for rights for self-determination removed. At the border of each of their communities, large signs declared that pornography and alcohol were banned. The Australian Army was mobilised to enforce the emergency measures, and the country silently watched on. Paedophilia, child neglect, substance abuse and domestic violence were broadcast as Aboriginal problems, never mind the effects of colonisation and prejudice; never mind that gender-based violence is prevalent across the entirety of society, and as we have learnt, rife in the very parliament where these decisions were made.

Indigenous men Australia-wide felt the stare of suspicious eyes, as many people believed that our children needed special protection from their own race, especially from their fathers. These attitudes were all based on lies.

And as a middle-aged father of five children, I saw a cartoon in a major newspaper, *The Australian*, that reinforced a negative stereotype about my capacity to be a dad. It depicted an Indigenous man, beer in hand, indifferently facing a police officer who held a Blak boy by the scruff of the neck. It implied that the man was the father of the boy, and because he was Indigenous he did not know his son's name, nor did he care for him. The cartoon continued the lessons taught to boys in schools. It reinforced the prejudice against me. Indeed, the cartoon was blatantly racist.

Racism is an attitude found in the shallows of the streets and shopping centres, through the thick midstream of the Australian media and our workplaces, to the dark depths of the decision-making state and federal parliaments.

It is against this tide of ignorance that First Nations

men defy racism, to love and care for ourselves and our families.

•·•·•

At the Perth Writers' Festival in 2020, I met Miles Franklin Literary Award-winning author, Tara-June Winch. We discussed books and publishing, and as Blackfullas invariably do, we talked about family, Country and connections. Tara suggested I write a book about fatherhood.

I considered the idea but wasn't sure if I would be capable of doing it, with all my flaws and because of the stereotype I had lived with since childhood. My mind was changed when I read James Baldwin's book *The Fire Next Time*. I was inspired by Baldwin's letter to his nephew.

The epistolary style, which is very personal and often sounds as it would if it were spoken aloud, I realised, would be an ideal form for Aboriginal and Torres Strait Islander men to talk to our sons and fathers, and to celebrate who we are.

I set about finding fathers and sons to share their perspectives.

The letters in this book by sons and fathers for each other are lessons about life and love, about culture and pride, about sexuality and race. Our letters are ultimately a celebration of Indigenous men, though importantly, in a book by men, we have written about the need to end harmful behaviours such as toxic masculinity, coercive control, misogyny and sexism. Men are undoubtedly the main instigators and perpetrators of gender violence. It is our responsibility to call it out among us, to never harm women again.

Each of the authors has been challenged by writing these letters. Each of us has learnt more about ourselves. Our writing has been healing.

I was also inspired by poetry by Indigenous writer Kirli Saunders and the young Indigenous poets in Alison Whittaker's anthology, *Fire Front*, and Desert Pea Media's, *Homeland Calling*, edited by Ellen van Neerven. And so in this book, I have included poetry and aphorisms as well.

With each page we wrote, we Indigenous men, have built a vessel. With the strength of our ancestors, we pull the oars of truth against a tide of ignorance and toxic masculinity. And with our words, as bright as the stars on a moonless night, we offer our children shining points of guidance. We have done it for our people and our Country – for our daughters and mothers – Indigenous girls and women, Indigenous people of all genders; we have done it for our non-Indigenous friends as well, so they may end colonial behaviours and take up an oar of truth with us – to go on a voyage to a better future.

Thomas Mayo

THOMAS MAYO

Zenadth Kes

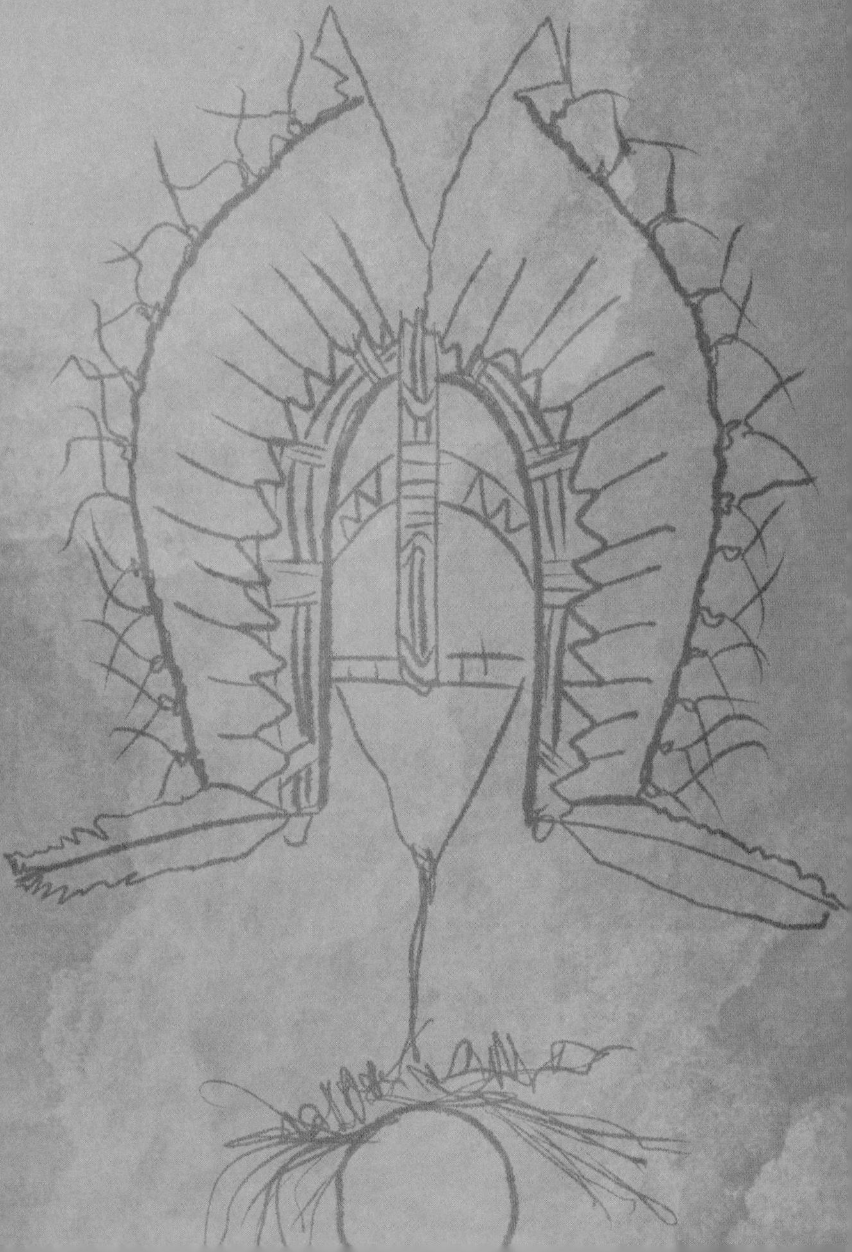

Dear Son,

Do you remember, when you were about nine, you tried to take my hand as you always did, and I said you were too old to hold my hand in public?

I wish I had never said it.

I now know that what I said was wrong.

At the time, I thought what I felt was natural, that when a son reaches a certain age, a father will feel awkward about demonstrating his affection for him. I thought this was how a father helped a son to become a man.

But what is it to be a man?

You are barely nineteen now and this question might not have crossed your mind. You've moved to the big city of Perth, concentrating on your apprenticeship. For the first time you are living away from your family, with new responsibilities. You are regularly cooking for yourself and your housemates, paying bills and keeping your home clean and tidy.

How are your cooking skills coming along? I enjoyed guiding you over the phone through cooking your first simur, or vermicelli chicken. You haven't called for help since.

But I have thought about it – about 'manhood' and 'fatherhood' – especially now that I'm raising young children again, with the arrival of your much younger brother and sister, William and Ruby, who are eight and six years old. I have wondered what shapes how we behave as men, and in particular, as fathers.

It is undeniable that our fathers shape how we father our own children, whether we are conscious of it or not, and whether we do it well or not. Above all, our understanding of being a man and a father is linked to our own father figures. This is especially pertinent to us – Indigenous men – who all have a mother and father, at least within a few generations, who have been terribly wronged – enslaved, raped and dispossessed.

Your Pop's generation were born under lawful segregation and the complete control of a white 'Chief Protector'. Pop lived in Queensland, the state that inspired apartheid in South Africa. His generation of young men were the first to throw off those shackles, but they remained bound by the walls of prejudice. His generation, mine and yours, we all struggle against a more subtle, more cunning systemic racist control. This, and more than 200 years of intergenerational trauma. These burdens are uniquely ours to carry on these stolen lands. To this ongoing struggle, for you and your children to come, I have dedicated my life.

With my obligation to the following generations in mind, I thought it would be good for you and me both if I were to write about fatherhood. Reading books and writing thoughts are wonderful things – I can hear you saying, 'Yes, Dad, I know, you tell me that every time we talk.'

'Our understanding of being a man and a father is linked to our own father figures.'

Well, son, this letter is my example for you. I will write to you about the behaviours that I once thought were acceptable for men – behaviours I now know are wrong. I will also write about the effects of historical trauma that I have passed on to you, and your sisters.

For good measure, I have invited some friends to write about fatherhood as well, because different perspectives are essential. I want you to learn to be a good man, a good partner to your loved ones, a good human being – and I want you to understand that there are more ways than one to do this, if you learn humility, empathy and how to love, the way our ancestors did.

When I told your Pop that your mum was pregnant, he shook his head and told me I was stupid, as he often did. I didn't fight him. I never did. I just walked away and got on with my 'stupid' life. I'd resigned myself to what seemed to be a simple fact about my relationship with my father – I could never do anything right.

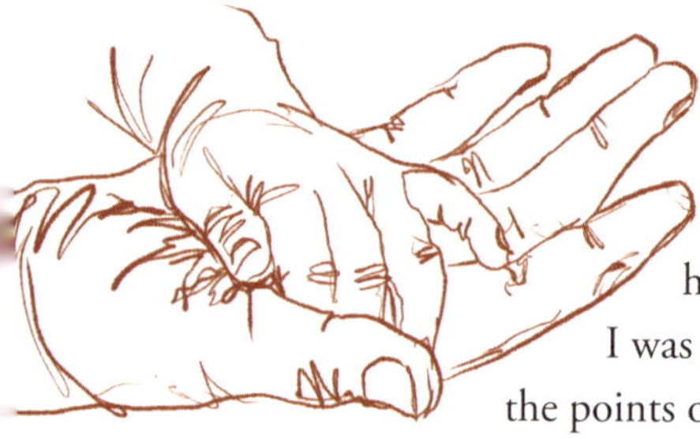

His reaction to this news hurt but I wouldn't be deterred. I was your age, still a teenager, and all the points on my nineteen-year-old compass were covered. I had the thrill of hunting at sea on the wide reefs around the Vernon Islands; a warrior's accolades on the rugby field; and in my infatuation with your mum,

I'd found the most luscious Garden of Eden – the magic of young love. There was only one other direction I wanted to go. I wanted to start a family.

Your mum and I met in Darwin only days after she had moved there from Broome. Our relationship quickly bloomed, our love soon becoming too great for my meagre room, shared with an unrelated uncle. We wanted privacy and a place to put down our roots. The best we could do was to move into a share house together with your mum's sister, Aunty Millie, and several other friends; having a room on our own was like living in a mansion back then.

We were the same as most young people, pitching in with other people our age in a challenging step toward an independent adult life. Son, you are also experiencing the joys of living with other young people who are new to life in a share house. You're discovering how supplies you were saving mysteriously disappear from the cupboard; or food that is not yours stays in the fridge and evolves until it has arms and legs. You're experiencing the impromptu parties and working out how to cope with throwing in for bills and the rent.

In my youth, I was fortunate to have started working on the wharf. My trade union, the Maritime Union of Australia (MUA), traditionally provided work opportunities for Indigenous people and for people of colour who had found asylum in this country. Opportunities denied elsewhere at times. The union saw to it that even a young

Torres Strait Islander man could earn good coin and feel safe. Coin enough to soon buy a new place.

Our first home as a family was a second-hand – or maybe fourth-hand – caravan. While it was half the size of the share-house bedroom, and half of that was taken up with your sister's cot, we thought of it as moving from a mansion to a castle, leaks, ant infestations and all.

Life was good. I felt at home on the wharf, and my workmates were my comrades. They taught me to stand up for myself and for others, to use my voice and to think critically about how the world should be. And there was a bonus: the seafood readily caught from the Darwin docks.

Before and after work I would fish and catch mud crabs. Silver bream caught on a light line in the cool dry season, barramundi inhaling lures in the steamy wet. This source of fresh food was especially helpful when your mum and I found ourselves in financial debt. We were not really managing our money very well. Some weeks we lived only on what I caught. If I caught just one small fish, I would make soup and rice so our bellies could be full.

That reminds me – have you used the hand reel and squid lure I sent you? I taught you how to hunt and fish, so you'll never need worry for lack of food, son, so long as you're on familiar Country. For us, this is always the sea. It comforts me to know you can catch and cook your own food.

I'm still amused when I think about you as a toddler, watching me getting ready to go to work. You always hovered around like a little puppy. You'd watch with your big eyes as I kitted up in my fluorescent-orange uniform and steel-capped boots, and you'd ask, 'Are you going fishing, Dad?' Perhaps you thought fishing was my work.

By the time I was twenty-three, all three of you older children were born, and you were all still babies really. I loved nothing more than coming home from work and you excited kids would welcome me as if I were the dawn and you were the chattering birds singing a loud, joyous welcome. As a new father, I marvelled at how you each had your own distinct character from a very young age.

Your mum had a long, hard labour when Shayla, your oldest sister, was born. At the time, I quietly implored the ancestors to always watch over her. She was born covered in vernix, a waxy protective substance, like wrinkles on a wizened Elder. As her character emerged, Nanna described her as an 'old soul'. She said, 'This tiny woman has been here before.' The ancestors listened, I thought. It was as though they walked with her; as though they whispered in her ear, at times.

Tiah, the happy-go-lucky girl, came next. She was a dancing flame of energy one moment, and the next minute, she would curl into a ball and play with her bellybutton while furiously sucking her bottom lip as she fell asleep, anywhere, anytime. Her moods changed as quickly as she entered the world – from first contractions to birth in under two hours.

And you. After two girls, I thought I would be the opposite of Uncle Jacko, who had ten boys. I was worried I would have all girls. I've learnt since that this should not be of concern. What you can enjoy with a child, and what a child can become, is not based on their gender.

You were the cutest and chubbiest baby I have ever seen. Your big kind heart beamed like a lighthouse, shining out in your smiles. Through a mixture of your personality and what you learnt by observing your sisters, who were always up to mischief and in trouble, you were an angel to guide through childhood. But then my cute chubby boy soon became a skinny, awkward, gawky teenager, just like I was. Regretfully, I felt our relationship change.

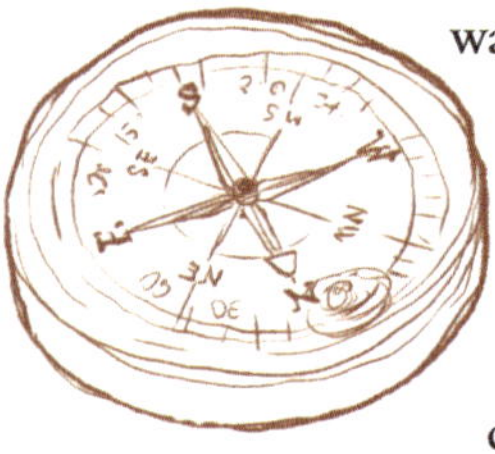

When I was a boy, there was a memory I would use as if it were a child's tattered comfort blanket. I'd pull the blanket out of a compartment in my mind after one of the many admonishments from your Pop. It was a vivid and happy memory of a time when my father had showed his love for me, holding me high above him as he spun around. I remembered the sensation of flying through the air, looking into your Pop's laughing face, while behind him, the pictures on the walls flew by in a blur. A moment of nonsensical joy and unbounded fatherly love. 'Why can't he love me like he once did?' I would ask those pictures on the wall, as I drank the salty tears that ran down my face.

There were other joyous moments with your Pop when I was a toddler. And it is not as though there have been none since then. My dad softened a great deal in his later years. But while I was growing up, such affectionate moments were few and far between. I treasure each one.

Your Pop often told me I was stupid, but I pretended I didn't care. It seemed I could never do anything right, and after hearing this over and over, my attitude was: If you think I am stupid, Dad, that's what you will get! I resigned myself to not even try to be better. My confidence became battered and scarred. To this very day, my confidence is like a shadow, impossible to coax out unless I am forced to step into the spotlight – and there it is.

As I said earlier, your Pop comes from a very different time. To understand him, we need to understand his past.

Pop was born and raised on Waibene (Thursday Island) in Zenadth Kes (the Torres Strait), near a tiny rocky island where only several generations before him, James Cook planted the British flag, falsely proclaiming the doctrine of terra nullius – that this continent and the adjacent islands were uninhabited. For thousands of years, that tiny rocky island was named Bedhan Lag. Cook renamed it Possession Island.

Cook not only lied, he also kicked off the invasion of all First Nations land on the great southern continent. When the six British colonies throughout the continent formed a Federation in 1901 – Australia, with the colonies becoming the states we know today – the first order of business was to segregate, assimilate and exterminate the Blak Indigenous peoples. The policy was aptly named the White Australia Policy. The laws made under the White Australia Policy were titled Protection and/or Preservation Acts. An ironic name for legislation enabling genocide. Under the Act, the white authorities could legally hold (and steal) our wages and our children. They could direct Indigenous peoples to work without pay or compensation. In other words, we worked as slaves. They controlled where we lived, who we married and where we could go. The practice of culture and language was forbidden. Your Pop spent his childhood living under this regime.

Pop's father was only forty-eight when he passed away. So, your Pop started working after his eighth year at school, which was as far as formal education could go on the islands. He had a great reputation for his work ethic. When he was seventeen, he left Thursday Island to work in a mine in the Northern Territory. He could barely speak English; Kriol was his first language – a mixture of Islander, Asian and English languages.

They were exciting times for First Nations people. A constitutional change following the 1967 referendum had achieved our full citizenship status as Australians. This was a catalyst for a resurgence of our pride. The land rights movement was in full swing and the *Racial Discrimination Act 1975* came to pass. Despite these great reforms, prejudice remained rife, yet your Pop managed to overcome it. We must not forget that his success came with great sacrifice.

Pop rarely gives voice to his culture and the prejudice he has faced. His attitude, I feel, is carried over from the times when our families were focused on surviving. His attitude has always been to work hard and get on with it. I have the greatest admiration for him because of this, while at the same time, I have seen how this attitude leaves too much unsaid. Perhaps it hurts him to speak of what he has gone through. Perhaps he has never healed.

Who knows how much of your Pop's harshness toward me was a result of the way society treated him? We will never know. He won't talk about it.

Son, for us to learn how to improve ourselves and the next generation of men, we can learn from our own feelings – what pleases or hurts us; what others do that causes feelings of jealousy or anger, and what affects how we trust someone. We can do better if we try to be perceptive and use empathy to improve how we relate to others.

We should keep an open mind to the underlying reasons for a person's behaviour. If someone has been abused as a child, for example, as an adult, they might struggle to express and accept love; or a child who is disruptive in school might not be naughty for the sake of it, but because of the impact of a mental trauma. And different from what I was taught when I was young, we should believe that a person's depression is real, and like other health afflictions, requires care. It's the same with poverty and powerlessness.

For fellow Aboriginal and Torres Strait Islander people especially, the effects of inter-generational trauma are a scientific fact linked to historical truth. It is intergenerational trauma and the conditions created by prejudice – the systemic and constitutional powerlessness of First Nations people – that causes high levels of Indigenous incarceration, domestic violence and poor health. The root cause of our plight is racism, not our culture or a genetic flaw in our DNA.

Ending gender inequality, toxic masculinity and overturning the patriarchy and white supremacy will help us change society for the common good. Connecting with our culture and learning to comprehend our feelings to reshape our priorities and how we care for others is how we can heal and become better men. It is how we will be better fathers. This we must do, for our children to come.

When you were growing up, I made a point of never calling you stupid. I didn't want to inflict the same pain I experienced. Though I wish I did better. During your childhood, I failed to make enough changes to my own ways. I said homophobic things and made sexist comments to deter you from being 'like a girl'. I'd tell you off for crying. And I called you a 'wuss' when you complained about being hurt on the footy field. I want you to know that my attitude to such matters was completely unacceptable.

You and I have both suffered from tapping into retro Australian culture. We have both lived with intergenerational trauma. We must continue the great efforts of our mothers and fathers. We will rebuild.

Your mum stayed home to look after you and your sister when you were babies. This was partly because I expected she stay at home to care for you, as Nanna did for your aunties and me, and because I wanted to be the sole provider. That was my misguided ideal of manhood.

Your mum was at home with three babies; she had no adults to talk to and all her close family and friends were in Broome. As a wharfie, my work hours were irregular. To find out what shift I was required to work the following day, evening or night, I'd telephone a recorded message at 5pm each day. We rarely planned time together.

Couples overcome challenges such as these and worse, though I believe now, we struggled because of my attitude. I wanted to party with my mates and was frustrated if I couldn't go out with them, so I would take it out on your mum. I was never physically abusive – Pop never raised a hand to Nanna and I never dreamt of doing so to your mum. On reflection, though, I realise I was emotionally immature. I would behave poorly, expect the impossible, and then make your mum feel like I was the victim. It was never her fault. The fault was all mine.

Our relationship spiralled into a miserable place. Though, while our love faltered, your mum and I always loved you children.

You were four years old, standing between your mother and me when we had our final argument. You were crying, confused and frightened by the intensity of the exchange. We were probably arguing over nothing of great importance. My misconception of manliness and my immaturity were more at fault than anything your mother ever did.

In the heat of the moment, I demanded that your mother go back to Broome where she'd come from. We had argued a lot leading up to that day. We were both unhappy. The following morning, your mother and you three children were gone.

When I came home from the night shift, the heavy silence in a house that had always been filled with the sounds of family life, was torturous. Toys lay on the floor like corpses. My footsteps seemed to echo between the walls as they had never done before. For weeks, on waking, I would reach across the bed, feeling for your mum's warmth, only to touch the cold sheets. I'd lay still and listen to the silence. No, I didn't have a nightmare. This is real, I'd think. What had I done? I constantly asked myself. I've lost my family.

In those first days of emptiness, I cried on my way to and from work each day. One day I broke down and cried mid shift. I went home to languish in my hollow heart. I imagine your mother had already shed her tears before I did, in the days and weeks when she was deciding whether

or not to leave. At the tender age of four, you likely bore witness to her pain – for that I am sorry.

When I started writing this letter, I had no idea where it would take us, son. All I knew was that I could teach you something by my example. And though I am aware I have been brutally honest about the worst of me, I don't fear you will think me a bad father. Like my father was for me, I was there for you from the day you were born. I worked hard. I played with you, kept you safe and loved you as a father should. I hope you will learn from my example, and how I chose to raise you and your sisters.

Several months after you and mum left, I had dusted myself off and suggested to her that she allow the three of you to come home. There will be more opportunities here in Darwin, I said. And though you kids were only aged four, six and seven, I was ready for the challenge. Your mum said yes, so long as I sent you back to Broome every second July and Christmas school holidays, so she could spend some holidays with you.

With you and your sisters back home, I took to doing all the tasks I had expected your mother to do. I had fun doing a terrible job tying Shayla's curly hair. I dry reached each time I wiped your butt. And I went so far as to starch and iron your clothes every day. After work, on rugby training nights, you kids would sit on the sidelines on a picnic rug with the dinner I'd hastily cooked, packed in

'Be kind, show empathy and keep an open mind. And always stand up for yourself, son. Stand up for your family and your people.'

plastic containers. You were all well-behaved. You would sit and eat your dinner while I trained, before I took you all home, bathed you and tucked you into bed. I made certain I provided plenty of hugs. There are no rules about which gender must do what.

I was wrong to think I should work and your mum stay home; or that I would cook the barbecue and your mum mop the floors; or that it wasn't my job to change nappies and launder the clothes. A partnership in parenthood should be as equals, as it is between Mel, my wife, and me today. You work it out together. Also, partnerships should not be exclusively between men and women – your sexuality is what it is. Love is love.

Writing to you about this has helped to teach myself. It has been like an antidote for the vestiges of toxic masculinity learnt from father figures, peers and western culture. I'm still unlearning.

While Torres Strait Islander culture is patriarchal, mistreatment of women and violence toward them in any form, is not. We care for our women and our women care for us. The matriarchs of our family, your Nanna and aunties, were always there for us in the eighteen months when I was caring for you as a single father. We love our children as a family unit, or before colonisation, as a clan. How else could we survive – an unbroken culture – for tens of thousands of years?

Family violence was learnt from those who invaded

our lands. It was amplified by poverty and generations of trauma inflicted by the colonial program of dispossession and racism. We did not rape our women, unlike the conquering white men did, as they systematically disempowered our men.

My son, I don't need to be a scholar to teach you what I know about fatherhood and manhood. What fatherhood and manhood is, is quite simple.

You should treat people the way you want to be treated.

You should listen to others – listen with your ears and your heart – and learn from their perspectives.

Be kind, show empathy and keep an open mind. And always stand up for yourself, son. Stand up for your family and your people.

I love you and your big sisters, and the little ones love you too. You, my sons and daughters, you mean the world to me.

We can't wait to see you in Darwin again – Ruby and Will idolise you. And I make you this promise: unlike when we last got together, when all of the above was weighing on my mind, I will let go. I will express my feelings, I will hold your hand and we will talk, man to man.

Love from,

Your dad

Fatherhood

In your eyes
I saw a new day dawn
As a twinkling star
An ancestor
Come thither and warm

First breath
Heartbeat
Burgeoning cry

Mother's relief

Tears in my eyes.

We follow the path of least resistance
until compelled by love.

Ailan dance

Thrumm, thrumm the warup humms
Deep like voices imbued of sea
Lifted skyward by song, mak-time and kulap
Raining down

Filling our hearts

Dancing our ancestors
Our Country
Our story
We

STAN GRANT

Wiradjuri

To my boys,

Listen to this.

Bumaldhaany Babin.

Listen to those words.

Each night I would drive past the Royal Prince Alfred Hospital in Sydney, wind down my window and yell those same words.

Bumaldhaany Babin.

My father – your Pop – was in the neurology ward, he had lost his speech and his movement. He had taken a heavy fall and suffered a severe brain trauma. The bleeding had formed a clot. He was eighty years old and there was no guarantee he would come back from this.

Bumaldhaany Babin.

The Bumaldhaany are our warriors. My father is my Babin. I knew that somewhere in that hospital, he could hear me. COVID restrictions meant that I could not see him in the Intensive Care Unit. Only my mother – your Nan – was allowed in. But my boys, he could hear me; I was sure of that. Our language would find him, and he would fight because that's what Wiradjuri warriors do: we fight.

Your pop had been sick before. He had already undergone brain surgery for a benign cyst. He had been in deep pain. Every part of his body ached and he suffered blinding headaches. In his quiet moments he had told my uncle he didn't know if he could go on. Or if he even wanted to.

The magpies came. Garru. He saw them in a dream. They were on the front lawn of his house and they were talking. The Garru were Dad's father and his grandfather. They spoke to him in our language and they told him it wasn't his time. There was more he had to do.

This was your Pop's mission – to save our language. As a boy he had spent time with his grandfather Budyaan out in the scrub. Old Budyaan spoke seven languages and he taught Dad his Wiradjuri. Budyaan yelled out to Dad one day in the main street of town and a cop heard him. The old man was arrested and jailed.

When he came out, he said he would never speak our language again. He saved it only for when Dad was with him, out where no white man could hear him. Your Pop spent a lot of years just surviving. Just putting food on the table. For Blackfullas, life was hand to mouth. One day at a time, one town after another, one backbreaking job then one more and one more.

Pop has got scars all over his body: scars of survival. Scars from the boxing tents; scars from the sawmills; scars from the coppers. Then there are scars we don't see; scars that he keeps hidden. Scars of the soul that don't heal. Your Pop is scarred from Australia.

There have been times he has been angry. When I was a boy, I saw that anger and sometimes I felt it too. I don't blame him now. It was all he knew. He had to save me from the life he had been forced to live. He had to make me tough and get me ready for the blows that were surely to come.

Other times Dad – your Pop – was just sad. I saw that deep well of pain behind his eyes. They were black eyes, dark pools of history. So much history, so much anger, so much hurt. And all we have left is us. Just us, holding ourselves against the world.

You never got to see that. Life has been easier for you. And I'm glad for that. I am so glad that you boys don't know what it is like to not know where you will live from one week to the next. You don't know what it is like to be hungry, or to watch your mother go to the charities and ask for help, for food. I'm glad you don't have my memories. And I'm glad I don't have my dad's memories.

You have seen the best of your Pop. You've seen a softer side of him. Isn't he beautiful? By the time you came along, he didn't need his muscles anymore. He didn't have to shape up to the world, he had survived and he'd found a way to speak back. His way. His words. Our words.

Bumaldhaany Babin.

Your Pop has given you the most wonderful gift. He has given you our language. Because of him, Wiradjuri is

‘I’m glad you don’t have my memories. And I’m glad I don’t have my dad’s memories.’

protected and preserved forever. He has written it all down in the Wiradjuri dictionary. A whole generation of people speak our language now because your Pop saved it.

That's what keeps him alive. That's what the Garru said to him when he was sick. It wasn't his time yet.

But we are losing him. I know we won't have him forever. And I'm scared, boys. I am scared because I'm not ready. I am scared because I'm not man enough yet to live without him in the world. I need him to fight just a bit longer to give me time to grow.

When he is gone, I will have to take his place. I will have to plant my feet in our soil and pull all of our strength from the earth. I will have to stand under the stars and speak to Baiame to ask him to make me a man.

We spend our lives preparing for this, my boys. Remember when you were young and we would drive from Sydney to Nan and Pop's house? Remember those long drives? We used to stop at Yass to get petrol and have lunch, not just for the food but because it marked the start of Wiradjuri Country: your Country.

Remember how I told you about the land? You would look at the rocks and the hills. I told you how the land dipped into a valley and rose on the other side: that side was home. You watched how the sun hit the trees and how the earth flattened out and how creeks cut across it like blood veins.

Home, boys. You have only one home in the entire world. One home that has always been there and will always be there. One home and a family: our blood in our Country.

This is how the world turns, my boys. We are born and we learn and we live and then we pass on. We learn from those who have come before us. I spent time with my grandfather when I was young. I used to help him inside when he came home drunk. I would collect all his loose change when it fell out of his pockets and keep it for him. Then I would give it back to him and he would take me for an ice cream.

I wish you had known him. My grandfather – my Pa – was the most important person in my life. He wasn't Wiradjuri, he was Kamilaroi. My mother's father, my mother's people. You have strong Kamilaroi blood too, my boys.

My Pa has been gone a long time. Sometimes it is hard to remember him: his smell, the touch of his hands, his voice. I imagine him now more than I remember him. But he is always with me.

Like me, boys, you will have to live a long time without your Pop. In years to come you will lose that sense of him. He will drift to the back of your mind. But he will always be with you. When you see the Garru you will see him. When you speak his words – our words – he will be with you.

You will live in a big world, my boys. You already do. You will love and you will have your children and I will try to be to them what your Pop has been to you.

We don't know where the world will lead us. I left our Country, I left our family and I went to other countries. I have seen war and suffering; I have seen people beaten down and I have seen them endure. I have looked into the eyes of people who have lost everything and I have seen the eyes of my grandfather and my father staring back at me.

It was hard for you in those years. Too often I wasn't there. I missed a lot but I had a job to do. And you will have your jobs to do and you will make your choices and live with your regrets.

But remember whatever happens, wherever you may go, however far from your country or your people, remember you have a home. You have a place in the world. You have a language that is yours. And you have your Pop – my father. His spirit will never leave you, boys, it will never fail you.

Bumaldhaany Babin.

Fight on, Dad. You're not done yet. I'm not ready to be the man you are.

Look at your Pop, boys, isn't he beautiful?

Love,

Dad

TROY CASSAR-DALEY

Gumbaynggirr, Bundjalung

Dear Clay,

I always wanted to be a father, ever since I was a boy. I always dreamed of being a good dad, just like my father was to me. When I was young, I would hold my little cousins, who were a few years younger than me, and think about how I wanted to hold my own little child like that one day.

I think these feelings stemmed from the fact that I didn't have a lot of continuous time with my own father, because my mum and dad broke up when I was twelve months old. My goal even as a child was to fix what I felt was broken about my own childhood and be there 24/7 with my kids.

When I met your mother, I knew she was the one from the minute I spoke to her. She was gorgeous and smart, and we made each other laugh, and laughter is very important to me; it always has been. I fell in love with your mum straight away.

Your mother and I had our own careers, but we were very much on each other's side as soon as we met. When we first got together, I was taken back to the dreams from my childhood of being a father one day. But I also realised I wanted to be a good husband too. I'd always hoped I'd find someone who was willing to work alongside me in an equal partnership in life; not to be a housewife but to follow her own career as well. Your mother was that kind of woman. She was driven, compassionate and we had each other's back all the way. Growing up with my mum, who

'My goal even as a child was to fix what I felt was broken about my own childhood and be there 24/7 with my kids.'

was a single parent, I always had huge admiration for strong women. I was surrounded by them because my aunties were strong as well. When your mother came along, I could tell that she was also strong and resilient. Saying what we meant to each other made my heart sing, and we bonded from that moment on.

After your mother and I got married, we'd often look at each other and say, 'What are our kids going to look like?'

'If they look anything like you, they will be gorgeous!' I'd say to her.

And I was right, you and your sister are gorgeous.

I would also say to my wife that we can't have only one kid. I was an only child and it was terribly lonely a lot of the time. After we had you, Clay, there was quite a gap before your sister came along. I kept nagging my wife, saying please don't let this little fella be an only child. I wanted to have a couple of kids, so we could be a little unit. And that's what we ended up with, and I'm very fortunate.

When you came into this world, in my mind I turned back into being a child again, saying to myself that my dreams will come true. And they did. I held you and thought, I get to be a father now and be responsible for a little human life. This was something I took more seriously than anything in my life before then, because I knew that I was about to help shape someone else's life. I wanted to always be there, to see it through.

As well as my dad, I had other male role models when I was growing up. They were in my Aboriginal family, starting with my grandfather, Henry Daley, and my uncles, Gerry Daley, Buddy Daley and Freddy French.

These men filled the gaps left by a broken family and gave me the tools to be who I am today, from teaching me to fish, how to hunt for witchetty grubs, and ways to fix a car or bike. They were always there to talk through problems I was having in my life at the time.

All the things they showed me about being a father were in my heart the day I first held you when you were born. I couldn't wait to show you all the things that made my life rich – culture, love, humility and the value of family.

Being a musician and working at night, I had the luxury of doing school drop-offs. Some parents dropped off their kids then drove to work. But I wanted to be more involved in your morning drop-off, so I started to play hand ball with you and all your mates before school. For most kids it would not be cool to have a grown man – your dad – playing handball with you and your friends, but you accepted me. I played like I did back at school and called out all the kids who thought it was okay to cheat!

I've since had some of those kids, who are now in their early twenties, come up to me and say things like, 'I remember playing handball against you when you came to school with Clay, and they were some of the best games we

'I couldn't wait to show you all the things that made my life rich – culture, love, humility and the value of family.'

ever had with no cheating!' Those words mean so much to me.

Words and actions can break the cycles that are hard for us in our lives. As I look back at the role models I had who helped me to break these cycles, they make me think about the role model I want to be for you and your sister.

Henry David Daley, my grandfather, was a railway worker and a proud Indigenous man who only thought about providing for his family. He had nine kids and he was able to rent an Aboriginal Commission home for all eleven of them. Eventually he got a loan to buy it, and he paid the loan off the week he retired from his job. In doing this he broke a cycle of having to depend on others, and broke down many stereotypes that were around for Aboriginal men of his generation.

I remember Pop as a quiet man. He passed away when I was nine and he was quite sick toward the end of his life. I often think of the hard times he lived through. His mother died early in his life and he was raised by a few different relations before he struck out on his own.

My mum recounted a story about Pop while he was working on the NSW Railways. One of his colleagues accused him of stealing pumpkins that were growing wild by the track near the railway yards at South Grafton.

The man said something to this effect: 'Typical thieving Blacks, taking those pumpkins.'

Well, my Pop heard this comment and proceeded to

walk over there and punch this bloke right in the jaw. He dropped him like a hot rag! Then he said, 'I didn't lay a hand on any bloody pumpkins, thank you.' And he went right on back to work.

Those attitudes were rife in his day. I think Pop wanted to prove people such as this man wrong by fitting in and working bloody hard. It would have been tough for all his generation, but he didn't wear the hardship like a badge. Instead, he just slowly changed people's minds.

I used to get a huge thrill when someone would say to me, 'My father used to work with your Pop on the railways and he said he was a great bloke and a great worker.'

These are the qualities I hope our whole family have inherited, and I always feel a huge amount of pride to hear these comments. I saw how my Pop, Dad and my uncles all worked hard to provide for their families, and I wanted to be like them.

I remember teaching you how to fish, just like my dad and uncles showed me, and the pride in your eyes when you caught your very first fish is locked in my heart forever. The simple things we inherit as boys from the menfolk of our families end up being so special when it's you doing the teaching as a father.

On the way through your early life, Clay, I worked on helping you to understand that humility, tolerance and accepting people as they are is important to making you the best human being you can be. When you were little, I encouraged you to share with your sister and your first cousins and not be cheeky to your mum or me. You and your sister got a smack when you were naughty, just like I did as a kid. I have no regrets about that because from a very early age you learnt right from wrong, and you've never forgotten it.

If I did something wrong, I'd get a smack from Nan or Pop, from my mum or from my uncles or aunties. No-one was immune from being pulled into line in our big extended family. It was all about respect – you disrespect someone, you get a smack. That's how it was.

When you were twelve, I took you to the Northern Territory. I had to do some shows up there and I wanted to bring along an old and ailing friend of mine, Brian Young.

I first toured with Brian when I was twenty, around your age. I was a young musician with big dreams, just starting out, and the Brian Young Show was exactly what I needed. It was nine months of travel right throughout Australia, mainly playing in very remote Aboriginal communities from Queensland to Western Australia.

By the time we reached the Kimberley in the Northern Territory, Brian had become a musical father figure to me. He impressed me for many reasons – first for his love for Indigenous people and the respect that went both ways, between Brian and our people. Secondly, he was very wise, even though he was just fifty-five when I met him.

Everything he said seemed to tell me that he'd lived five lives in one already – being a rodeo champ, a ringer on stations and then an outback entertainer. His values as a man were something I learned from, and the musical lessons he gave me about stagecraft are skills I still use today.

During those nine months away with Brian, I learned a lot about traditional Aboriginal culture and lore, and I have so much respect for them. I also came to understand the importance of family. I went away a naive boy and came back a man. It was like a musical initiation and a rite of passage that so many musicians had done for years before me.

I stayed in close contact with Brian for many years, getting him in for shows, paying homage to him on stage as a role model, and acknowledging the things he imparted to me. I gave him the respect he deserved.

When I took you to the Northern Territory, I asked Brian to come too. He was quite old and frail by this time and I wanted him to have the chance to see his friends up there in Gunbalanya for the last time.

He needed assistance to get on and off the plane and, Clay, you learned on that trip how to be patient and to have respect for your elders. It's not that you didn't show any respect before, but on this trip in particular, it was a really important lesson for both of us. You came up to the Territory with me and fitted in with all my old friends and their kids like you'd known them all your life. I also felt like I'd given Brian something small in return for all the wonderful things he gave me, which I've carried on into my life as a father.

You were always an old soul; my mum and aunties said you had been here before. Your sister Jem, on the other hand, was carefree; a little solemn at times but usually she doesn't have a care in the world. She's the best little sister you could ask for.

I'm so proud of the people you and Jem have become. Your mother and I look at you both and shake our heads and say how lucky are we to have two grounded, humble and compassionate kids who have grown into caring adults.

Now you are twenty-two years old, living in your own little unit with a mate, and you have a steady girlfriend who is wonderful. I hope you've seen the respect I have for your mum and it makes its way down the generation into your relationships. You have seen your mother and me share a laugh, have a good time. Maybe sometimes we fight over little things and big ones, but we've got through to where we are today by having respect for each other. There is no such thing as a perfect relationship. If someone says they've got through life without a bump in the road, they're kidding themselves; that's not the way it works. But I have to say, by staying with your mother I've broken another cycle in our family – that was another thing I wanted to fix about my own childhood. We have stayed together as a family under the one roof, and that was my goal from the get-go. I'm proud to say we are still here as a family, still respecting, loving and caring for each other whenever we need it, and that's probably the most important thing. We cherish having each other in our lives.

Clay, fatherhood is a beautiful commitment that will never leave me until they put me to rest. I am so happy and proud to be dad to you and your sister.

Dad

Learn from your children

A child is curious about difference, not prejudiced;
eager to learn, rather than ignore.

We can learn from the innocence of our children.

The world as it should be

Children imagine the world as it should be.

It is up to us to make it that way

for them.

The turtles cry
for sandy islands melting
inhuman tides

Listening is a language

Listening is a language
We cannot understand
Until ears and eyes
Connect to heart and spirit
And time is suspended
To feel

Yessie Mosby

Kulkalgal

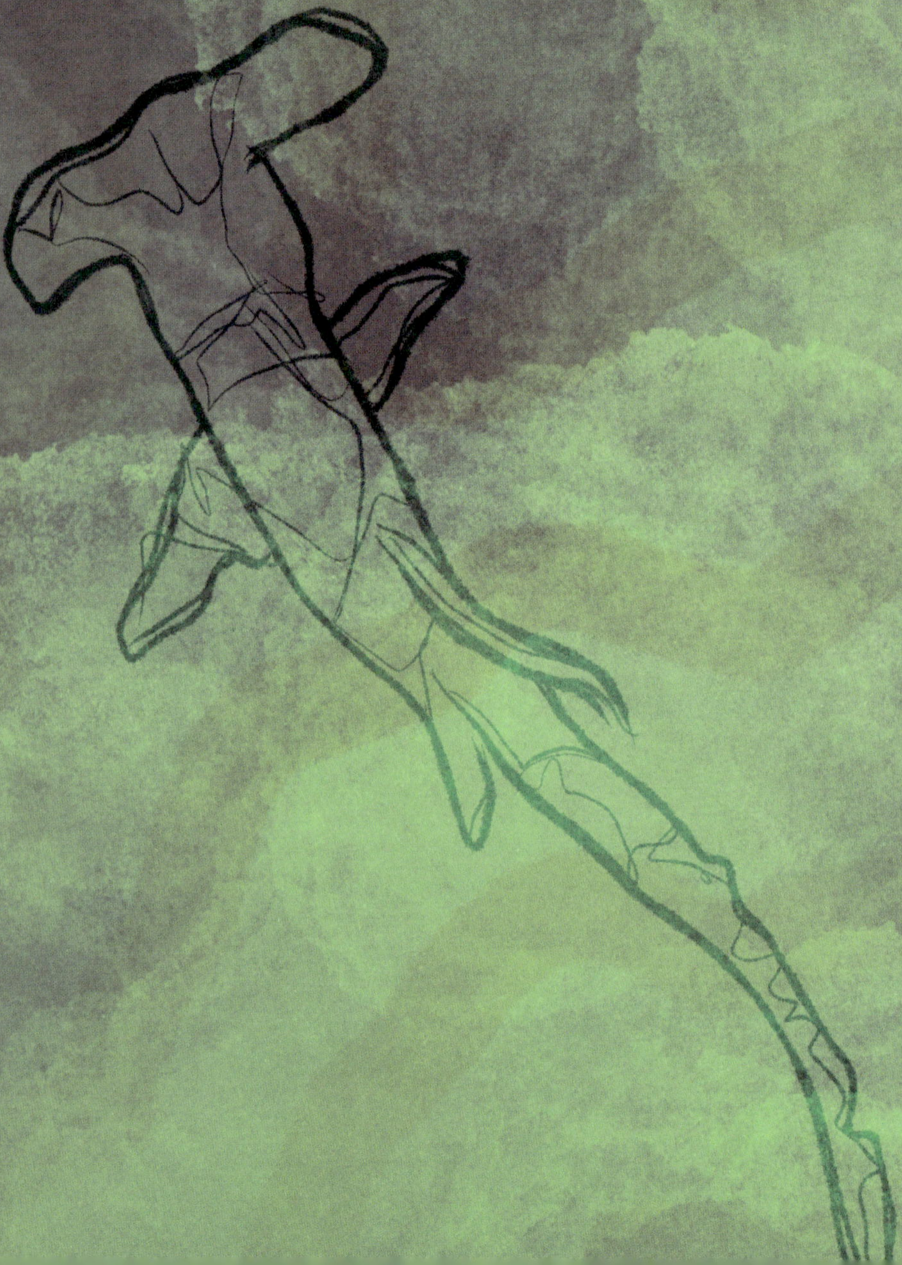

Dear sons,

I thank God for blessing me with four strong young warriors, my sons Genia, Awara, Santoi and Beimop. I've never written a letter before. This will be my very first and it's written from Masig. It will be a memorable letter because it's for you, my sons. I write this letter thinking of our island home of Masig. I think of the sacred place where I feel most at peace, Genian Payai. Genian Payai is the burial ground where my sixth-generation grandfather is buried. Genia, my eldest son, you were named after him. I call this place home. It gives me peace, just like you do. May this sacred place always be your home too.

Coconut palms surround this area. We eat the fruit hanging from the native trees here. I'm sitting under the shade of the coconut trees, listening to the wind as it whistles through the leaves. I can see crystal blue water. Shells are in abundance. Where I sit, when the water hits the beach mark, you can see little pippi shells. They dance as the waves come in and out. As the tide changes, they go back into the sand. When I look at that, it makes me happy. I hear the ocean; it washes and cleanses my mind. I think of you, my sons.

I sit here knowing that I am guided by the spirits of our ancestors. Butterflies and dragonflies fly around me as an indication that they are with me. I think about when I was a young boy, growing up in the village when my grandparents were alive. It was happiness. Most of our days were spent down in the water with my cousins.

My grandparents would call us turtles because as soon as we woke up, we followed the tide to swim. We ate musu, the succulent inner fruit of a sprouting coconut, for lunch. We ate almonds and fruits from the bush. We ate fragrant witchetty grubs called kuparr, the larvae of moths. We drank coconut water. We would follow the tide like turtles, just like you do, my sons.

When we were young, we were turtles playing in the tide, but as we grew older, we turned into goannas. Our duty was to keep the yard clean and cut the branches of the dangerous trees with a machete. As goannas, we were taught how to collect turtle eggs. We were taught how to walk out onto the reef to collect fish. We would sit with our wadhuwam (uncles), who taught us how to make rope and how to splice it. They taught us how to cut the cassava and replant the stems. We'd go diving from the dinghies, observing our uncles who hunted dugong and turtles. At that age, our duty was to gut the turtles.

We had a lot of ceremonies. When we caught our first catch of fish with a spear, we would have a ceremony. A first catch would mean a big feast. Either our matriarch or patriarch would have the first bite of the first catch at this feast. My sons, you have experienced these rights of passage. You are turning into goannas.

When we were young, we didn't have electricity. We had pressure lamps. We had to go into the bush and collect firewood to light the boilers to wash our clothes. We had to learn how to make fire. At night, we would husk coconuts to burn to create a bonfire. We'd throw paiwa (sandalwood) onto it and it would produce a sweet scent and chase away the mosquitoes. Our parents and grandparents would put woven matts out for us to sit on under the stars near the bonfire, and we would listen to ancient myths and legends. I try to continue this tradition with you now, so that you can pass these stories onto your children. It is also my obligation to release you to your wadhuwams, so they can teach you everything you need to know about life too.

Genia Wilfred Markerr Dajil Mosby, you are ten years old and you are the eldest. Awara Smith Gethe Mosby, my second son, you are five years old. Santoi Allan Terra Mosby, my third son, you are four years old. Beimop Eldridge Kebisu Gelam Mosby, you are three years old. I gave you names in our Zenadth Kes ancestral lineage, passed down for hundreds of generations before Christianity arrived. The names I gave you are from within our bloodline. I don't want our bloodline ever to be forgotten.

When you see a flock of birds flying as an arrowhead in the sky, you will see the leader at the front; that leader is called Yathai kuik. Where that bird turns, the flock follows. If that bird goes in the wrong direction, he has an impact on the flock. My father was the Yathai kuik of the Mosby clan. The first son is the Yathai kuik, the leader of the flock. My father and his father's descendants were the Yathai kuik; a long legacy that stretched back over generations. When my father died, it was my responsibility to become the Yathai kuik of our clan. Genia, as my eldest son you are the first in line. One day you will be the Yathai kuik. You will be the bird that flies directly behind me in that arrowhead. If anything happens to me, you will replace me as the Yathai kuik. If I die tomorrow, regardless of the fact that you are ten years old, you will become the Yathai kuik for our clan and you will be guided by your wadhuwam. Genia, when you were one year old you had your first ceremony. You have many more ceremonies to become Yathai kuik. All cultural protocols will be passed onto you by your wadhuwam.

Awara, Santoi and Beimop, you are Genia's bones. You are Genia's spine. You are Genia's ribs. You are his flesh. You are Genia's eyes and his ears. You are his shadow. You three sons will support Genia as a koom. 'Koom' in our language translates to 'a stick that has a fork'. We use this forked stick to support a banana tree when it has heavy fruit. In this life you will have each other. Awara, Santoi and Beimop, you will be Genia's koom. You will help him carry his load, because Genia will be like the banana tree. He will have a lot on his shoulders. As Yathai kuik, there will be times where Genia will struggle.

Genia, your brothers will be your support, helping you to stand up. When I pass on from this world, all the responsibilities will immediately rest on your shoulders, Genia. Your cultural responsibility will be to the extended family, the clan and the tribe as Yathai kuik. You will be the spokesman. You will carry everything on your shoulders, including traditional knowledge. It will be very stressful at times.

The four of you must help one another. If one forgets, the other will remember and remind them. If one is emotionally broken, the other one will lift him up. I love you, my sons. I have deep affection and respect for you all and I know that for you to live abundantly in the future, you will need each other. My four boys – you mean the world to me. I have so much pride for you. I know that my legacy, my clan and my teachings will live on through you. I will have four warriors to carry on my name, blood and traditions.

My sons, we are a people who have ties to the land, sea and sky. We are seafaring people. We are saltwater people. Our genealogy lies in the Straits – our ancestral remains are not only on land but also in the seas that surround us. Zenadth Kes is the name we give the Torres Strait Islands and waters. Zenadth Kes feeds us, provides for us, protects us, and it has done so for tens of thousands of years. We must look after our island, the way it has looked after us. The bosom of this land is our mother, and the water surrounding it is our father. We have to protect them. This world is changing rapidly. Every year the tides change. We see the seas wash Masig away. Erosion and rising sea levels are affecting our island home. We are picking up our ancestors' bones as if they are shells, due to the inundation of our burial grounds. Life is different now. Today we are affected by climate change. Your father is fighting for you to live a happy life on your island home of Masig. Genia, Awara, Santoi and Beimop, as your father, the sixth-generation bloodline Yathai kuik for our descendants, our

'I know that my legacy, my clan and my teachings will live on through you.'

clan, our tribe, I am fighting for your future. I am fighting for you to reside in your home, for you to be proud Torres Strait Islanders.

I love you, my sons. I fear for your futures if nothing is done to protect our island home. Regardless of the fact that English is not my first language, I will do anything to protect Masig for you and your children. If I could go back in time, I would sit with my Elders, your great-grandfathers, to discuss how we can plan and deal with what we are facing today due to climate change. The people of the world burn oil, gas and coal, and dump waste into our ocean. I want you to understand that side of the world.

I want you to see that the world outside of Masig is different. That world is affecting us. They made the mess but I want you to learn how to clean it up. I want you to learn how to survive on our island home and to save your home in this climate. I want you to balance your Indigenous cultural side with non-Indigenous ways of life, because we here in the traditional world don't have the infrastructure or tools to save our island on our own.

In 2019, I along with seven other Torres Strait Islanders became claimants for the landmark 'Our Islands Our Home' climate justice case. We took a climate change complaint against the Australian Federal Government to the Human Rights Committee of the United Nations. This case is the first of its kind in the world, supported by Gur A Baradharaw Kod, ClientEarth, 350 Australia and Seedmob.

I wanted to be a representative because of the love I have for you, my children. As a Yathai kuik, I'm not ashamed to speak my mind. I will speak boldly when it comes to my people, my culture and tradition. What I am trying to do is for your sons and daughters and the generations that will come after you.

I hope the Australian government will hear our cry. I hope they will see the problems that we face and act upon them immediately for the safety and survival of our ancient race. I hope Australia drops their greenhouse gas emissions, because we are suffering in the Torres Strait due to climate change. To make big money through mining and exporting fossil fuels to other countries while neglecting us is shameful.

This campaign was designed to tell the world that there are people living on specks of islands throughout the Torres Strait, on specks of islands throughout the Pacific and on specks of islands throughout the world, who are suffering great loss of their land and their home due to climate change. It is affecting all of us saltwater people – our way of life, our culture and our traditions. Where God has placed us, let no man move us away from our island homes.

In 2023, I with a group of Torres Strait Islanders within this tribe and neighbouring tribes from the Torres Strait will take part in a voyage never done before. A voyage in protest. It is a voyage where the world will stop and look. It is a voyage that will carry a lot of pain and pride for those we are representing. We will sail from the Torres

Strait down the east coast of Australia to protest against the government for its inaction regarding climate change.

As your father, you mean the world to me, my sons, and I will do all I can to protect you and your island home. When I wake up in the morning, I think of you; when I go to bed, I pray for you. I have picked you up and dusted your knees when you have fallen over. I will always be here as your father, your guardian, your protector and your provider.

My totem is ngagalaig, the eagle. If God takes me home, I will still be here to guide you, protect you, love you and nurture you. When I die and you see an eagle soaring in the sky, always think of me. When we see problems, we fly high and study the problems. We fly above the storms. Whatever problems are in the community, we fly high to study the situation. When we make our nest, we make it to withstand cyclones. The nest we make is the nest for the next generation and for generations after them. As the eagle, our responsibility in life is to provide for and protect our children. You will need to become ngagalaig, my sons. We as eagles, we fly, we soar and we overcome our problems.

These are words from your father,

Yessie Mosby

Yessie Mosby is a part of the Kulkalgal tribe. His letter was written from the coral cay island of Masig (Yorke Island), situated in the Arafura Sea. Masig is located in the central part of the Torres Strait, an hour away from the mainland of Papua New Guinea.

CHARLIE KING

Gurindji

Dear Dad,

You left us in 1985, aged seventy-eight. You and Mum were married for fifty-four years, and you lived for only six months after Mum passed away. I think you started dying the moment she did. In my grief for Mum, maybe I never mourned you properly.

As I reflect on your life and mine, I am left with sadness for what we didn't say. As I grow older and understand myself more, I feel that I come to know you better. It is small comfort, but it brings me warmth that I can honour your life.

I needed to write to you to let you know how badly I felt about not being able to grant you your last wish. When you whispered to me to ask the nurse if you could have a smoke, I knew they would say no, and they did. They said it was because you were on oxygen and it would be too dangerous. I regret I couldn't say yes. I wonder if I should've tried harder to grant you this dying wish. You had done so much for our family and for others.

I have never forgotten how I felt when I found out you had lung cancer. I knew you had smoked all your life but it never entered my head that it might be killing you. When my sister told me, I went numb. She said, 'I got some bad news about Dad.'

Before I could ask, he said, 'He's not going to be all right.'

I remember now how some months before my sister told me, I had heard you having a coughing fit and I wondered if you were okay, but I dismissed the thought and didn't worry any more about it. Maybe I should have suggested that you go and see a doctor. Maybe I didn't because I always thought you were invincible.

Mum, a Gurindji woman, was the great storyteller. We lived through her stories. Your stories seemed wild and so far from my own experiences. So wild that I suggested you should write them down, so we could have some type of record of your life. In early 1983 you gave me 183 pages of handwritten notes. They were stories from your heart and your life, about being a pioneer, about caring for your family, and making the most of what life had dealt you. I was grateful to have a written account of the stories, though I did not read it until many years after you were gone. It was then that I realised I has missed an opportunity to really know you.

Your memoirs, that you titled 'Jack King: My life in the Territory', raised many questions. Your grandchildren ask questions too – questions I don't know the answers to. I would like to have asked more about the things you did while you were working in the Territory, the people you knew, and the way you could put your hand to anything. You were never afraid of a challenge or hard work. Most importantly, you were defiant of the norm back then. You were a white father who loved an Aboriginal woman as an equal and stuck around to raise your Aboriginal children.

I think the Malvern Star Australian bike adventure was your most legendary endeavour. In 1926 you were approached by Sir Bruce Small, the owner of a small bike shop in Melbourne. Bruce had invented the Malvern Star bicycle, and he wanted a bike rider of your repute to promote it by riding around Australia in an attempt to break the previous record of seven months and twenty-eight days. Already an established rider at the Sandringham Bike Club in Melbourne, you relished the chance to take part in this epic journey on two wheels, and on 30 September that year, you and a riding partner, Basil Nixon, hit the road.

Forty-seven days later you arrived in Darwin. From Melbourne you rode up the east coast to Brisbane, then west to Mount Isa. Onwards west and into the Northern Territory. Almost at Katherine, at a small community called Marnboy, your riding partner Basil Nixon shot himself in the leg.

Unbeknownst to you, Basil had hidden a gun in his riding trousers. He confessed to you later that he carried a weapon because he was afraid of the Aboriginal people – he thought we were cannibals. When Basil hit a ditch and fell off his bike, the gun went off and the bullet became embedded in his leg. What a ride that last few hundred kilometres must've been for you, with Basil struggling beside you, with a bullet wound. When you made it to Darwin, Basil was shipped back to Melbourne and you decided to stay. You didn't want to ride on without a riding partner. You had ridden 4500 kilometres and fate would soon deliver you to your future wife.

Stuck in Darwin, you started working on the roads. But the heat and humidity were overwhelming, and you got sun stroke so bad you went to hospital in a coma. When you became conscious, you opened your eyes – and this is how you tell it – there, standing by your bed was an angel. You thought you had died and gone to heaven, and the angels were Aboriginal. Mum, of course, denied the romanticism of your story, but you'd say, 'How would you know what I was thinking?'

You ended up getting work in transport, driving a six-tonne Leyland truck throughout the Top End, delivering supplies. There were no proper roads or maps, and you'd often have to dig your way across creeks. You'd also have to load and unload the supplies. You did this for four and half years, and later told me that it was some of the toughest work you ever did. I think about this and picture you as a vibrant young man and a hard worker. Over the years, you became well known as a truck driver, driving some of the first trucks with trailers in Central Australia – they were known as road trains. You drove an eight-tonne Matador that had eight-wheel-drive, with front and back steering and a winch to lift and replace the tyres. It was so strong, it coupled up to the three trailers, the same as a train. The road train you drove is now in the National Road Transport Hall of Fame in Alice Springs.

'You were a white father who loved an Aboriginal woman as an equal and stuck around to raise your Aboriginal children.'

I look back on your words about the hardships and challenges of driving trucks through the Northern Territory and into Western Australia, the connections you made, the knowledge you gained. You opened up the Territory and made roads where there were none, all in order to deliver much needed goods and materials to remote cattle stations. What you did was remarkable. How come they never named a road after you? Probably because you were not a blowhard and you despised people who were. Perhaps because you refused the prejudices of the time.

Mum, Ningardi, was stolen, along with her sister Maggie and their friend when they were young, because they were half-caste. Mum was only eight years old. She was living with her family on the edge of Limbunya Station, at a rock hole that was a special place for the Aboriginal people of the area for many thousands of years – there was water in it all year round. Mum could only speak Gurindji when she was taken.

As a child, her job around the station was to pick the fruit and vegetables. She told us how much joy she got when she would ride the station's horses.

When she was taken, Mum said she was picking watermelons in a fenced-in plot. Mum and the others saw three horses coming in from the east. It was a police officer and the native welfare officer with a packhorse to carry the kids away. They had been tipped off that there were half-caste kids there.

They took Mum to the Kahlin compound in Darwin, an assimilation facility. They renamed her and the other two girls, and separated them so they wouldn't speak their language to each other. Mum's new name was Ruby Jane Smith. Her sister was named Maggie Smith, and the other girl was named Daisy.

When Mum was eighteen, she got a job at the hospital. That's how she ended up beside your bed – your angel.

After you passed away, I went to the rock hole and found the place Mum was taken from. The fence was still there – dark, rusting wires lying in the dirt. As I took in the scene of her childhood and the tragedy of her kidnapping, I saw a vision of her returning with you, when you refused to follow the rules and decided to take Mum back home. You returned her the same way she had left, on three horses. You and Mum rode your horses to that place with a packhorse following behind. I wasn't born back then, but I wish I could've witnessed it.

At the rock hole, Mum got the shock of her life – her mum was still there. And her mum knew you from when you drove trucks, yet only in that moment did the connection become clear. I can imagine the tears that were cried that day. Tears of joy. A reunion that no-one ever thought would be possible.

Dad, I reflect today, and I think this is the greatest love story ever told. I was so grateful that you took Mum home, so she had the rare opportunity to be reunited with her family. You probably didn't realise the significance of that journey. Mum's return to her home helped us to challenge history and change our story from one of victimhood to survival. I know that it changed your story too.

When you told your family in Melbourne that you had married an Aboriginal woman, they said you were never to bring her home. You didn't have any contact with them again after that. We were proud of you for standing up for Mum and our family. It came at great cost for you, but for us it defines so much of who you were. Loyal and a man of conviction. Later, I was proud that you encouraged Mum to meet her father, a white policeman who was living in Adelaide.

Our family – by then there were four children – went on that trip to Adelaide. It must have been an epic venture because, at the time, you were all living at Wave Hill. The trip included trains, planes, cars and taxis. On arrival in Adelaide, you made arrangements for Mum to meet her father, who by then was the police commissioner, William Francis Johns. She met with him for just fifteen minutes, the bare minimum. He gave her twenty pounds and that was the end of it. Although she never really spoke about it, we knew it was an important thing for Mum to do. Though it didn't go so well, she was never bitter. She often told us kids, 'Don't get bitter, get better.'

I wish I could have thanked you for arranging that

meeting. By doing so, you showed us how much you valued Mum and in turn how you were proud of us and who we were as Gurindji people. I never told you how significant these actions were, how they shaped our family and how much we admired you for being so committed to us all.

I always saw myself in Mum's image. She was Aboriginal and I am Aboriginal; this identity is who I am, what I know. It is how I feel and what I believe. Mum was the main figure in our family, fiercely maternal, resilient and strong for her children.

While I had two older distant brothers, I was raised alongside my many sisters, always feeling special and cared for. Mum didn't want to lose me to your world, Dad. You and my two brothers, Les and Reg, seemed like some other-worldly heroes. We would look forward to your arrival home and you never let us down. You would bring us mangoes, coconuts, paw paws, sacks of peanuts, and other treats. Your homecoming was also a time when all my misdemeanours for the year were corrected. Mum had a list.

Sometimes I didn't entirely welcome your visits because you would put me to work. You taught me how to do jobs that would help Mum, such as killing poultry, doing the garden, chopping wood. But you would leave again and our lives would return to normal, and I would go back to my somewhat privileged positioned as the only male of the house. I sensed that for my mother this life was probably hard and lonely. Our finances were unpredictable and Mum

'I always saw myself in the image of Mum. Defined by her history, the injustice of being removed so brutally from her people, her land and her language.'

had lots of responsibility. I know you needed to be where you could earn good money to support us, and that it was a big sacrifice for both you and Mum.

I'll never forget that time in Alice Springs when you took me, a teenage boy, out to get a killer. We drove south along the railway line, eyes peeled for a bullock. You patiently explained to me that my job was to look after the bullets and keep them separate from the gun. We had the bag for the offal and the knife and steel ready. I excitedly pointed at a bullock standing in the shade of a tree, so pleased to be the one who had spotted the beast. You turned the Wolseley around, lined it up and took one shot.

Sitting alongside the carcass on the trip home, I thought sadly about the bullock and my role in its demise. I knew then that to become like you wouldn't be a natural progression. But, of course, I wanted your approval. When you lined up a mechanic's apprenticeship for me in Alice Springs, I went along with it, although my heart was really in other things. Playing drums in my band, The Scene, and hanging out with my gang of friends, the Midnighters. I don't think I was ever going to follow in your footsteps. I remember your disapproval when I was playing drums in Zedena's, the little restaurant on the banks of the Todd River. You walked up to me and said, 'Is that all you do – bang these things?' In my mind I was Ringo Starr, rings on my fingers, feeling proud. Soon after that I quit the band.

I know you were worried about me, who I would become. After your years away, you were concerned about your teenage son. I know you didn't approve of me being part of a gang as a teenager, you couldn't see the sense in it, but I did it anyway. Your disapproval when I got a tattoo was stinging. I know you were thinking I had been too protected by my mother, too coddled. I started to feel then that living up to your expectations was going to be hard. Could I be the man you wanted me to be?

Dad, I am who I am. I always saw myself in the image of Mum. Defined by her history, the injustice of being removed so brutally from her people, her land and her language. But I know, too, that I am definitely your son. Like you, I never seem to stop. Maybe I'm not building a windmill, but there's always an urgent task that needs doing as a journalist at the ABC. Like you, I am always trying to do the right thing.

I want to tell you about a special moment I had when I was covering the boxing at the 2012 London Olympics. I was waiting for the crew to cross to me and my mind went back to 1958 when I was sitting on the floor by your feet and you were listening to the boxing on the radio. The bout was between George Bracken and Aldo Pravisani for the Australian Light Weight Title. My memory was of you quietly supporting George Bracken who went on to win, with the glow of a cigarette on your face. When they crossed to me, I could barely speak. Tears rolled down my face. Your memory put a spell on me, a small reminder of how powerful memories are; how they can comfort you and bring you closer to someone, even after they are gone.

I'm wondering still whether you had a happy life. With eleven children could you really know us all and could we know you? You set the bar high and for that I am forever grateful. The great revelation to me, even if tinged with sadness, is that I still have the chance to understand and learn from you through your memoir. It helps me when I sometimes wonder, What would Dad do?

I never told you how much I admire you. I regret that I never told you how much I love you while you were alive. I hope you are proud of me.

Dad, I love you.

Charlie

BLAK DOUGLAS

Dhungatti

Dear Dad,

It took me your lifetime, I regret, to be able to put into words my sentiments and emotions. Why didn't I say more when I stood by your side at the Nepean Hospital, as you took your last breath?

I've since wondered about the way we males stop showing affection around the time we reach our early teens. It perplexes me. Was it an unwritten law in the western suburbs of Sydney where you raised me? I remember how it was: to be seen hugging one's father at school drop-off demonstrated 'gayness' – God forbid! And to so much as kiss one's dad on the cheek – no way. Holding back on affection was like damming a river. It was nothing short of emotional torture, a ridiculous homophobia. Australian society was a veritable microcosm of toxic masculinity – impeding the development of Homo Sapiens. Perhaps that's delving a little too deep? I can see you raising your eyebrow and smiling wryly now, Dad.

You and I were the epitome of chalk and cheese.

I am Blak Douglas, an artist. I make a living with my paints and canvas. I fight a racist system through creative expression. Art has helped my river flow.

You were Bob. You made a living labouring. You fought against racism with your fists and brawn.

You were born in Thubbagah (Dubbo), in north-western New South Wales, around the time of the Second World War – an era when some Blakfullas were still being neck shackled and chained to trees. You were born only two

'I fight a racist system through creative expression … You fought against racism with your fists and brawn.'

decades after the most recently recorded massacre of First Nations peoples on this continent.

I was born and raised in the suburbs of the big city of Sydney. I could go to university, yet in my lifetime, the neck chains were swapped for handcuffs. First Nations people still die in police custody with no justice; Australia's grossly disproportionate incarceration rates do the colonising work that the massacres once did.

In your school photos, you are the only identifiable Koori amongst a dozen white kids. Your dark brown skin and piercing blue eyes made you stand out like a cheetah in a chook pen; they said you had speed like a cheetah too. You told me you were popular, until one day, a kid used the term 'Boong'. It must have been hard for you, once you learnt what being a 'Boong' meant to all the other kids around you.

So how did that pan out for a young, handsome Dhungatti Aboriginal warrior?

'Wanna 'ave a go, yer black bastard?'

Into your adulthood, the racism continued. Each time you entered a pub, the shenanigans would begin. It is this vicious cycle that sadly still rears its ugly head today, usually in the country town establishments and on the footy field.

And so, the Blak man is against the ropes once again.

Only way out for you was to fight. No wonder we are good with our fists.

You lived your young adult life knowing that when the end of the week came, and you were looking forward to 'beer o'clock' at the local, 'shit was bound to hit the fan'. Especially when you had eyes for the hot young barmaid. Dilemma being that she was white.

The barmaid you fought for became my mum.

You were a hard man, Dad. I still marvel at what you went through in your life. You worked from when you were eight years old. As a boy you did multiple jobs – driving trucks, working at a cannery – and after hours, helping your mum clean the bank. You collected soda bottles on the weekends with your sister, Dianne.

In my childhood, I remember my biggest worries were simply keeping up with the trends.

In the early 1980s, the BMX phenomenon was sweeping through the state, and the race was on, literally. My head was in the clouds, dreaming of bikes like Quicksilver, DG and PK Ripper. Dreaming about bikes, styling my hair, popping zits, and wearing over and over the only 'cool' shirt I owned, believing it would give me the best chance I had of finding a girlfriend, kept me busy. Child's play while you and Mum worked yourselves to the bone.

In adulthood, they gave you a new nickname, 'Black Bobby'. It was better than being called 'Boong'. And it was said with respect. They say your work ethic was legendary. You showed them all up when Black Bobby started a business – Boomerang Excavators. While Mum worked nights, still in Blacktown a long way from home, you would operate your backhoe all day with a commute that had you gone from sunup to sundown. I remember Mum prepping your dinner on the stove before going to work, so you only needed to heat it up when you eventually arrived home.

When your truck required repairs, you actually drove the backhoe to and from the job. It still amazes me that you drove a tractor with a top speed of 50 kph along the roads, leaving home at 4am in the middle of winter, covering a round trip of some one hundred kilometres. You would come home at night, shower and eat dinner, clear the dishes and then sit and tutor me until I could complete my times table. Yet I would still protest. I was oblivious to what you and Mum did for me.

Your work ethic saw to it that you and Mum were able to buy a home in Western Sydney in 1978; there were no other Blakfullas who owned a home around the area back then.

There are so many reasons I admire you, Dad. It was as you said, and I remember this saying with affection now that you are gone: 'It's not often I am right, but I am never wrong.'

You were a numerical wiz and a crossword aficionado, which was quite astounding considering you only ever read the *Daily Telegraph*. Another trait I found captivating was your handwriting. You executed words on the page like a surgeon carving into flesh, your grip was both manly and magical. Watching you write, one could not see the end of the pen! Yet these beautiful cursive words or numbers flowed freely across the page. The more I think about it, the more incredible it was. You never typed on a keyboard. You lived for seventy-four years and while you would eventually own an iPad, you only ever wrote letters on paper, and performed long division like a mathematics professor, without using a calculator.

During tax time, when you did your own accounting, Mum often said that if you had put your mind to it, you could have been a top accountant. A statement that didn't equate because, let us not forget, we were in the late 1980s and within our demographic, Aboriginal people weren't accountants. Discussing this with my mentor at university, Aunty Jean South, she explained the harsh realities of surviving as a Koori in them days, and how there was a practical reason, Dad, why you chose to become self-employed, working in veritable isolation. Nonetheless, I thought you were a bit of a 'Rain Man' the way you would go straight to paper to solve any quiz I threw your way. You always kept the score when we played golf because you enjoyed it. Suited me.

I recall when I entered high school, I bought a 'starter kit' for mathematics and received a hi-tech Casio calculator equipped with a multitude of buttons up top that no-one really used. According to you, in the wrong hands, these things could easily exacerbate laziness.

'What are you going to do if the battery runs out in the middle of an exam?' you'd ask me.

One of my fondest memories about our relationship was from the time when you were a recent member of the septuagenarian club. Against your advice, I'd hastily got a mate to drive me all the way to Cessnock to lay down ten grand on a used V-8 Commodore station wagon.

'Dad!' I said, 'it'll be perfect for my school art-show tours!'

'Yeahhh, right,' was your reply, with your unrivalled tone of inflection.

There was no way I was going to leave Cessnock without that metallic green machine. I haggled at least enough to pay for fuel to get there. A test drive around the block and I was sold. What a dream to drive this thing back to Penrith. CD player! Tape deck! Air-con, six-speed manual, 5.7 litres and cruise control! After only ten kilometres, I had already devised the modifications plan.

Back home, after spending $113 at the fuel bowser, I pulled into the driveway, giving a few unnecessary revs to announce the arrival of the chariot. You walked out, adjusting your track-suit bottoms like Louis the XIV adjusting his sword. You began assessing, ducking and leaning in, then returned to the front. Hand to chin, you lowered your scrutinising gaze. Keeping your head at the same altitude, you took several paces back...

'She's been in a head-on.'

'Bullshit, Dad!'

You leant in, pointed to the left-hand edge of the bonnet, then the front left indicator, pointing out the differences in the gaps. It wasn't until the following year, when I had some repairs done that the mechanic validated your astute observation.

‘My hero,
my protector,
my warrior,
my educator,
my father.’

'It's not often I am right, but I am never wrong.'

I miss you and Mum, Dad. I didn't notice what special times we had. In fact, I was all too oblivious, until Mum suffered a stroke.

My heart melted when you became Mum's full-time carer. The love you demonstrated – the level of care you gave her was deep and constant. You took it on the chin and shook it off, for her, just like you did in your younger days when she watched you from behind the bar.

It wasn't until I observed this monumental relationship shift that I realised it was the same level of care you'd given me when I was a small child. I only wish I had shared this observation with you when you were alive.

Dad, you deserved a bravery medal. I certainly hope that wherever you and Mum are now, you can coexist in harmony, and that the pressures of life that weighed you both down daily are forever gone.

I truly miss these moments with you…my hero, my protector, my warrior, my educator, my father.

Perhaps in heaven there is no unwritten law against showing each other affection – two men – and even if there is, like down here, some laws need to be broken.

Your son,

Blak

Por kazil ya cam

Dato moon
Spik lo mi
Wene mama earth
E gad fertility
Mama earth
Lo nursery
Sustain ole life
With humility
Stars e shine
Old people be
Guide yumi path
Faithfully
This is our way
Blo land
And blo sea
Por kazil ya cam
Through eternity

An English word

noun

noun: colonisation

1. the action or process of ~~settling among and establishing~~ *murdering, raping, poisoning, starving, impoverishing, enslaving, assimilating to gain* control over the ~~i~~Indigenous people of an area.

   "~~Africa~~ *Australia* boasts a tradition of higher education institutions that ~~predate Western~~ *inflict* colonisation" *on Indigenous peoples*

   o the action of ~~appropriating~~ *stealing* a place or domain for one's own use.

   "the complete colonisation ~~of television entertainment by reality shows~~ *of Indigenous peoples lands, seas and culture*"

   o ECOLOGY

the action by a plant or animal of establishing itself in an area.

"lower airway bacterial colonisation"

Discovered in an English dictionary

DANIEL MORRISON

Noongar, Yamatji, Gija

Dear Son,

To be asked to take part in such a meaningful project, to be asked to write a letter to you is an honour and a privilege that I accepted without hesitation. This letter gives me the opportunity to share with you the life lessons I have learned, the legacy I aim to leave for you and, of course, to express my endless love for you.

As your dad, I am here to teach you about the things that matter in life, the things that don't, and how to tell the difference between them. I am here to make sure you feel loved and to teach you how to love others; I want to help you to know who you are, be proud of who you are, and also to be able to accept difference. In your short span of life, you have already shown me how you display this capacity to accept others. At such an early age you have had to think about and process topics that most kids won't ever have to, such as having a dad who now proudly identifies as gay. In response, you've only shown how understanding, accepting and loving you are – things many adults find difficult to do.

This letter is primarily for you, my son, but I also want to represent and act as a voice for other Aboriginal fathers who are gay, and write this letter for their sons, to let them know that each family is different and that's okay.

It is only because of the love and support you and your sister Mikayla have shown me, and the supportive family and friends we have in our lives that I feel comfortable

'In that moment, you proved to me that learning I was gay was something you were indifferent to. You didn't even flinch.'

talking about my journey. I will always try to be honest with you, and I encourage you to always be honest with me, as I will never judge you.

In comparison to many other men who eventually find the courage to come out to their family and friends, I had it relatively easy. I was met with love and support, especially from you and Mikayla, who mattered most of all.

I remember the day I made the decision to have the 'coming out' talk with you. I was extremely nervous and unsure whether I was doing the right thing. I understood there was no right or wrong time to tell you, and I knew it had to be done sooner or later. I took you down to a park near home, it was a lovely day with blue skies – a great day to be out with you and your footy. It was pretty much just you and me at the park; us, the birds and the tadpoles in the pond we sat by. We yarned like we always did before I eventually told you that I am gay. In that moment, you proved to me that learning I was gay was something you were indifferent to. You didn't even flinch. You just carried on being my son. Our relationship did not change one bit.

I'll be forever thankful to you for that. Clearly, it was harder for me to tell you I was gay than it was for you to know that I am. This was proof that you were comfortable in your own skin and not insecure about difference. You embraced it wholeheartedly, demonstrating maturity way beyond your age. Over the years, you've continued to show me and the world that having a dad who is gay changes nothing. I know it didn't change your love for me, or mine for you. For this, I feel eternally blessed and grateful.

It is sad but true that much of the world could learn from your acceptance – including myself. For years, it was at the back of my mind that I might be gay, but, afraid and uncomfortable, I chose to suppress my feelings and thoughts. I was trying to conform to the expectations of society, even though my own dad is gay.

Your Nan and Pop divorced when I was six. Soon after, Pop lived with his partner in the same home, but separate rooms. He didn't come out the way I did, because he lived in different times. In Pop's day, gay people were ostracised and physically abused for who they were. Our sexuality is as uncontrollable as if you are born with big feet or small, yet it was illegal for us to be ourselves. We couldn't marry the person we loved.

Pop's lived experience helped me, though I was no less concerned to come out. He was the first person I spoke to. I was as nervous as I was when I talked to you – the words fought to stay buried inside me, but I dragged them out. Son, there are moments in our lives when a bond with a loved one can be strengthened to the point of being unbreakable. This was that moment for your Pop and me. He shared his own experience, guided me through the positives of coming out and what pains I could expect.

The most encouraging lesson he taught me was cultural. Our family, our community, our people, they accepted him for who he was, and he told me they would accept me as well.

One thing I feel especially proud about is how our community has always been accepting of our family members who've come out as gay. In my experience, our community across the country has been very supportive and open to difference.

My experience is international as well. In 2012 I had the opportunity to visit Canada, where I met First Nations leaders, who are also known as Aboriginal. They told me how they consider First Nations people who identify as gay as Two Spirit people – incorporated into the First Nations community and respected for who they are.

Looking back at what I have learned from this, I want you to know that the most important thing is to be true to yourself. If society's expectations require you to deny who you are, then change the expectations of society. Do what Gandhi suggests: 'Become the change you want to see in the world.'

My attempts to suppress who I truly was had a negative impact on my mental health and general sense of wellbeing. I suffered from episodes of depression and anxiety for many years. My mental health improved once I had come out publicly in my mid-thirties. I consciously decided to be true to myself. I would no longer deny my sexuality. I had accepted that I was gay, no longer hiding who I was. That healed me.

'I want you to know that the most important thing is to be true to yourself.'

Being gay does not define me. I am still a proud son, brother, uncle, cousin and mate. I am a strong advocate for rights, justice and equity for our Aboriginal community and the wider community. Most importantly, I am still a proud dad – full of love, understanding and gratitude for the miracle and blessing of you and your sister.

It was not long after your mum and I were married that you were conceived. You can be assured that you were born out of absolute love, and you were a true blessing to our little family. You were our 'Bubba', and even though you are now in your teens, you are still our 'Bubba' and will always be. I just couldn't resist the temptation to name you Daniel after me. Of course, you were a welcomed addition to the family. Your mum and I had our girl, Mikayla, and our boy, you, and I was so proud and in love with you both.

I have told you and Mikayla many times that I wanted to 'freeze' you when you were very young, between two and four years of age. These were the most beautiful years of my life. Seeing two little humans developing your own personality and character. I wanted to keep you so small and cute forever. I have such amazing and beautiful memories of you, my son.

I am so grateful that I have been able to continue being a dad to you and Mikayla. You may be too young to fully understand, but in the past twenty to thirty years, some gay fathers haven't been so lucky. The gay community has had to campaign for the right to be free, safe and proud of who we are, just as Aboriginal and Torres Strait Islander people have, and still do. Thankfully, the world is now moving in the right direction. But I want you to know that our progress has only come about through our courage to stand up together to demand it.

Just as I did, at an early age you experienced your parents separating. I understand it was not easy or the best experience for you, my son. I want you to know that although your mother and I are no longer married, we will forever be connected and strongly united as parents to our two beautiful children. We will always be family.

Fast forward to my late thirties, I have a lifelong partner, Jason, who has happily accepted you and Mikayla as his own children. Jointly now, Jason, your mum and I are co-parenting; we're nurturing you to be the best you can be as a young man in this massive world. We hope to enable you to achieve everything you wish for and dream of.

In a way, you are lucky to be growing up with two dads and a mum. You could even end up with three dads! How is that for choice? You can choose which dad to take down to the park for a kick of the footy. I hope one of your dads will be worse than me at that, since you always make fun of my kicking style.

You and your sister have some amazing sports skills and talent that I cannot say I ever had myself. The way you are drawn to sports, and are so talented, comes naturally to you. I only wish I had been the same when I was growing up. It is safe to say you did not inherit the sporty gene from me. But I get a lot out of watching you play footy and basketball. You have a great passion for sport and fitness. I hope you continue down this track, as it will be good for you well into the future.

Like me, you have grown up remarkably close to all your mob and it is clear you are so proud of your family, culture, and connection to our beautiful Country. You are always proud to fly the Aboriginal flag at Aboriginal rallies and wear the Aboriginal colours. Our Aboriginal family accepted me when I came out. I am so thankful they supported us.

When I think of the person you have grown into, I feel extremely proud. You are someone others are drawn to and love being around – that is why you make friends so easily. You are kind, thoughtful and honest. These are great qualities, my son; they will serve you well as you continue your journey to adulthood and throughout your life.

You may not know this, son, but I am inspired by your determination and drive. Do you remember the time when you were learning to ride your new bike? The bike was so big and you were so small, but you did not let that bother you. You got on and fell off many times. After each fall, you would try a different angle or approach, and although they were not successful, you never got disheartened or gave up. Eventually, you found your balance and rode away with confidence and a huge smile that I will never forget.

You have continued to do this with every challenge you face. You display the courage and resilience I sometimes forget to have. Thank you for reminding me to never give up.

Throughout my career I have taken on leadership roles within the community and within organisations. I have dedicated my career to working with, and for, our Aboriginal community of Australia. I have chosen to do this as I see a lot of our people are still heavily marginalised and disadvantaged within the wider community. It is disheartening to know that our people are only winning the race in all the wrong areas, such as over-representation in the criminal justice system, in the out-of-home care system where children are taken from their families, homelessness, hospitalisations, chronic health conditions and low life expectancy.

Mostly, though, I have been dedicated to the plight of Aboriginal affairs throughout my career so you will not have to. My wish is that you and Mikayla do not have to continue to fight for justice for our community the way your grandparents and their grandparents and I have had to.

Son, the main thing I want you to take from reading this letter, is to have a solid sense of humanity, compassion and empathy for all peoples and communities, and commit to doing whatever is in your power to improve the lives of all and make for a better world. I promise I will continue to guide you on your journey.

There are simply not enough pages in this book to share how much you mean to me, but I truly hope this letter demonstrates how proud I am to be your father and how much love I have for you as my son.

Just remember that my love and support for you is unconditional and it is forever, my son.

Love,

Dad

JACK LATIMORE

Birpai-Thungutti

The Past We Step Into

Son,

I began to write this as an uncle, a great-uncle, my favourite great-uncle, waited for death to cart him to the next place. Weeks later, I have returned to finish it, after having rushed home to Country to sit with him as he left and his body closed down. I wrote our names on the box he was cremated in, and a note saying something like, 'Travel well, Uncle. You'll still be walking with us for a while yet, though.'

There were some things that occurred around the time of his death that I want to document. It's important that somebody else knows about these things, that you carry these things forward with you. I wish you could have made the trip with me, son. First of all, it was a marathon drive to get back on Country after the borders opened again at the eleventh hour, following the COVID-19 lockdown. That was one of the first two remarkable things to happen. The other was Uncle, on FaceTime from his death bed, propped up on pillows with a can of his favourite beer clutched in his hand, wheezing and semi-conscious, asking me when I was coming home.

If he didn't ask, I wouldn't have gone, and it dawned on me as I headed for the border in the inky early hours of morning the next day that he knew it. I cursed him and loved him a lot on that seventeen-hour run home, my eyes blearing out of focus and shifting sharply back so often I feared I'd drift off the motorway and be greeting Uncle at the next place when he got in.

The other thing of note occurred just south of Karuah in New South Wales, just south of our Country too. My tired eyes and highway hangover had forced me into a rest stop again. It was dark up there by that hour, but still early in the night. I called your grandfather and told him I was a couple hours off arriving at his house, asked did he want me to grab a dozen beers from Bulahdelah. Then Cuz called, said, 'You better get here quick. Uncle may not get through the night.' So I drove another three hours straight, as fast as I could, no more stopping, except to collect your Pop. We rolled into Port Macquarie getting on midnight.

It wasn't just the dark that made it hard to find our way, the town had changed. The roads and streets were curbed with gutters for one thing, and roundabouts punctuated proceedings where once it had been a straight run. It wasn't just me either. Your Pop got us lost too. And while we were repeatedly backtracking, spitting curses and trying to pull up screens on smartphones with absent signals, I was hoping all the while that Uncle was still holding on.

We were close but had taken a wayward right turn down a dark, deserted street in an industrial zone. An unmarked cop car followed us and flashed its lights. I climbed out from behind the wheel, phone screen glowing in full view, your Pop swearing and thinking the worst was about to unfold.

'I want time to stand still ... always in my arms and me always strong enough to carry you as far as needed.'

'My uncle is on his death bed,' I said before either officer could fire from the hip. 'I'm lost, but the map says we're close. Like 510 metres close.'

No sooner had we evaded the gunjibuls, than your old Pop led us on a full-blown home invasion. In the dark, the street numbers painted on the new curbing were not clear, and your Pop guided me into the driveway of a house with three other vehicles parked out the front.

I cut the engine after parking on the house's front lawn. Your Pop opened the front door and was walking down the hallway when I spotted the photos on the wall just inside the door. Suddenly it occurred to me that we might not have come to the right house.

Son, at this point I want you to know that you have helped me get through some pretty tough times. You need to know that I couldn't have done that without you. I wouldn't have got through what I needed to get through. You helped me just by being in my life. The night I married your mother, I told this to a hundred people crowded into our tiny backyard. You were two years old. I swept you up and spoke while holding you in my arms. How could I have done it honestly any other way?

I want time to stand still. For you to always be the age you were then, or the age you are now; always in my arms and me always strong enough to carry you as far as needed. It was the same with your older sister. It will be the same with your baby sister too. These are strong and common things for fathers to feel and wish for. I want time to stand still: this is a yearning so persistent, so much stronger than I felt as a young man. Time doesn't stand still though, and facing a startled stranger and his terrified wife in the dim, narrow, photo-lined hallway of that house that night, I felt the moving on of time was fortuitous.

Like time, everything then happened so quickly. There was surprised swearing; rushed, violent threats; hasty apologies; lively advances; quick retreats. No doubt the gunjies were called and our recent acquaintances likely radioed: 'Home invasion under progress in your area. Two perps, both male; the first described as grey, possibly blind in one eye, wearing shorts and thongs; the second also grey, heavily bearded, reeking of highway coffee; also wearing shorts and thongs. Vics report both perps muttering darkly about death beds.'

We piled into the car, which fortunately fired-up first go, just as the larger of the home-owners reached in behind the front door for a cudgel. I was sufficiently present of mind to avoid reversing over their water meter as we made a brisk exit.

Son, I am proud of you. I am proud of you for many reasons. I am proud of you for who you are right now, at five years old. Already, I'm proud of you for big, important things, but I'm also very proud of you for lots of silly stuff too. I'm writing this to read to you now, in the present, to let you know how much I love you, to let you know that

'Son, you have that same history as Nan and Uncle, and there's a defiance in you that's as immediate as your pulse.'

you're doing great just being you. But there are also things in this letter that are for you later, for a future you. And later still, when you're the age I am now, and years beyond here too.

I'm proud of you for so many silly things it could easily fill ten letters. And the size of my pride for all those things is – as you and I say – bigger than a whale's house. As well, I'm reminded every single day of the big things that make me proud of you.

In the playground in Port Melbourne on the Sunday before I left for Uncle, I watched you make new friends out of strangers. You talked to one kid there who was a few years older than you. You told him your name and then proudly and matter-of-factly informed him that you are special. He asked why. You said, 'Because I am Aboriginal.'

There was also the time when, within the first ten minutes of starting at your new kindergarten, you proudly told your new teacher that you are Aboriginal. Let me tell you why that is so important, why seeing and hearing that makes me so proud of you, and why it travelled with me – in my mind – home to Country to see Uncle.

I was around eight years old, playing on a steel hand railing on the edge of the public bar area at the Port Macquarie races. I could see the rust-coloured dirt the town was known for now covering the concrete pathway, a patchy slope that descended gently to the lush grass of the racetrack below. A white-painted timber and wire fence stretched along the last furlong of the home straight. The elongated mirror of the winning post glinted under the sun. It was towards the end of the day, hot as a blaze, and my mother was sitting on a bench talking to my great-grandmother.

I wasn't listening to them; instead, I could hear the buzz coming from the packed bar. There was the smell of beer and cigarettes and deep-fried fish and chips. But then my Nan and mum's close conversation speared through the din and I heard my Nan say she was proud of my mother, proud of me and my younger brother, because we identified proudly as Aboriginal. We were not ashamed of being who we were. 'You've done a great job,' my Nan told my mother.

This was in the mid-eighties, only about 30 minutes' drive south from a place called Kempsey, one of the most notoriously racist regional towns; racist against Aboriginal people. A place that is intrinsically woven into the fabric of our family. It shaped our lives and continues to resonate through almost every aspect of who we are. Below Port Macquarie's postcard gloss, it wasn't much different there either. It remains that way today, I can tell you.

The racetrack is close to Uncle's house. The streets in that pocket of Port carry names related to horse racing. There's Newmarket Grove, there's mention of Ascot, and a Doncaster Avenue. These days the streets that aren't related to horse racing – the newer blocks that have sprung up in the last fifteen years or so recall sailing, with names like

The Jib, Bosun Lane, The Boom, The Tiller, The Beam, The Mainsail. These kinds of street names are glorious banners of achievement for some people.

Beyond the racetrack, Uncle's house and the new subdivisions of land with the colonial street names, there is Hastings River. A road that used to be an unsealed track runs east–west along the riverbank. At the end of that track, heading west, was where our family lived – my mother, my great-uncle, my Nan – out in the swampy flood plains of the river, a long way out of town, away from the 'respectability' of Port. At the end of the unsealed road was a dirt track that ran through low-lying paddocks until it reached a weather-beaten shack. That's the house our family was crowded into, Blak and wild, and where, as a boy, Uncle walked to school.

There's a story I'm not even sure anyone else remembers anymore. It's about Uncle having the opportunity to stay at school even though he was older than the age the school was usually prepared to accept Aboriginal kids. It's not an old story. It's a yarn from the early sixties, so for many of us it's within living memory.

Uncle went barefoot through early primary school, but towards the end, as part of the conditions for him to continue, he was made to wear leather shoes. Starting out, he went through a lot of pairs of shoes. This was not because of the long walk up the track and down the unsealed road along the riverbank to get to school. It was because, after leaving home appropriately shod, Uncle would invariably pull up along the way, remove the shoes, and toss them into the mangrove creeks.

Each time he'd cop a terrific hiding, at school and at home. There was really no option but to wear the shoes. The leather shoes were the future that was open to us after nearly everything else of ours was taken away. At the racetrack, Nan saying she was proud of us was important to me because for our mob, not long ago, being Aboriginal wasn't something we were permitted to be proud of.

Son, you have that same history as Nan and Uncle, and there's a defiance in you that's as immediate as your pulse. I see it. I can also see qualities in you that already show me that you will do important things for our mob in your time. You will keep history to account. You might not always win, but you will always keep your opponents busy. That strength is in you.

I recognised it easily when you were still inside your mother: the way you would zip and zoot around inside her, waking her up late in the night. I'd be writing or reading something and she would yowl awake, then place my hand all around the dome of her belly so I could track you squirting about like a slippery prawn, all sharp little elbows and heels.

I'm proud of you. Carry that with you. And there are some other important things I need you to carry too, so that you, like your sisters, know who we are and why we are. These things are memories, but they are also futures. We tell these stories, speaking of how we lived – sharing our grief, our hope, our strength and resolve, having our pasts and our futures walk with us.

I once tried to write down every memory I could so that your big sister would one day know me well, walk with me if all went bad, travel well. I can't say why I thought anything would go bad, or why I would travel on early, but there you go. I wasn't even thirty years old, and I was still a decade off meeting your mother.

I wrote my memories down late at night in the unlined pages of a heavy notebook. My young family slept and the plump night hours elongated into the skinny, patchy grey of morning like the leopard-slugs that crawled over our kitchen window sill back then.

My daughter's mother laughed at me when she heard about my writing. 'How ridiculous,' she scorned.

In the notebook there was an entry about a woman who your sister and I saw on a West Preston tram. The woman was riding along in the tram with a boy, perhaps her son, or maybe her grandson. He was swinging from the overhead bars, jumping up and down on the seats, and screaming non-stop. Your sister was frightened. The woman's face looked so tired, but each time the wild boy came within reach, she would touch his cheek and the boy would calm down for a spell.

Another entry was about my father taking me to the Magic Mountain theme park on the Gold Coast in the early eighties. We rode the chairlift from the gate to the faux castle that had been plonked on top of the promontory. I recall looking along the famous strip and seeing what seemed like endless cranes lifting towers into the sky. Your Pop said the cranes meant a lot of work for him. The coast was riding an economic wave. I dropped a thong on the chairlift and when we got back down to the ground I had to hobble about with one bare foot until we found it.

Your Pop used to tell me a story of when he was a boy. His dad, your great-grandfather, used to drive a lorry. This was before people here started calling them trucks. Your Pop was headed home from school on a bus. There had been some troubled waters at home. His dad had been gone from the house several months after an argument with some interfering in-laws, who were also his neighbours. Your Pop said he was staring out the bus window, missing his old man, when he heard a lorry honking. He spun around, looked out the back window and saw his old dad waving, making hand signals for him to get off the bus at the next stop.

I wrote the memory in my notebook, and followed it with an entry of riding shotgun in my dad's metallic orange Fairmont. The stereo cranked out Bob Dylan's 'You're a Big Girl Now', as it kicked up cracker dust while it flashed down back roads between the town dump and a freshwater creek, Logans Crossing. The Dylan track was live and electric, recorded in the heat of the mid-seventies. Dylan was snarling with the accent, phrasing and expression that have always reminded me of Uncle and your Pop singing along at the top of their lungs, windows down, humidity in the eighties gushing in, hot tins of black rum rolling on the floor as we careened around loose-gravel corners.

I wrote that for your sister, but I'm writing this letter to you, son. You already know me, know I'm the old dad making signs for you, know already where it is all headed.

I was up the mountain looking over our Country, the way north, the way south, right along the coast. It was the day before Invasion Day. I was having a quiet, reflective moment, cursing all the Flaggies that had infested our lands below. I spent an hour up there, then came down and headed towards Port Macquarie, towards a motel room that we were using as a base to cover the next day's demonstrations.

The call came as I rolled past Christmas Bells Plains. Uncle had left while I was up the hill. I ended the call. Dylan's Dead Man jumped back into the car's speakers, while the plains that Uncle had asked to be buried on slipped by silently on my right. Country of our futures and pasts.

Jack

Son, when your partner is upset, you don't always need to have an answer, solution, justification or explanation.

Sometimes, you need only listen and give them a cuddle.

Let your heart lead

Keep Country –

the place, your people, your totems – in your heart

And do as your heart tells you.

always in a box or compartment or room or
building on a screen or page

longing

for Country, where the Ancestors vision isn't
cloaked by the fog of artificial lights and my
story can be written by footprints in the sand
where the tide the sun and moon is

eternal

JOEL BAYLISS

Gudanji, Wambaya

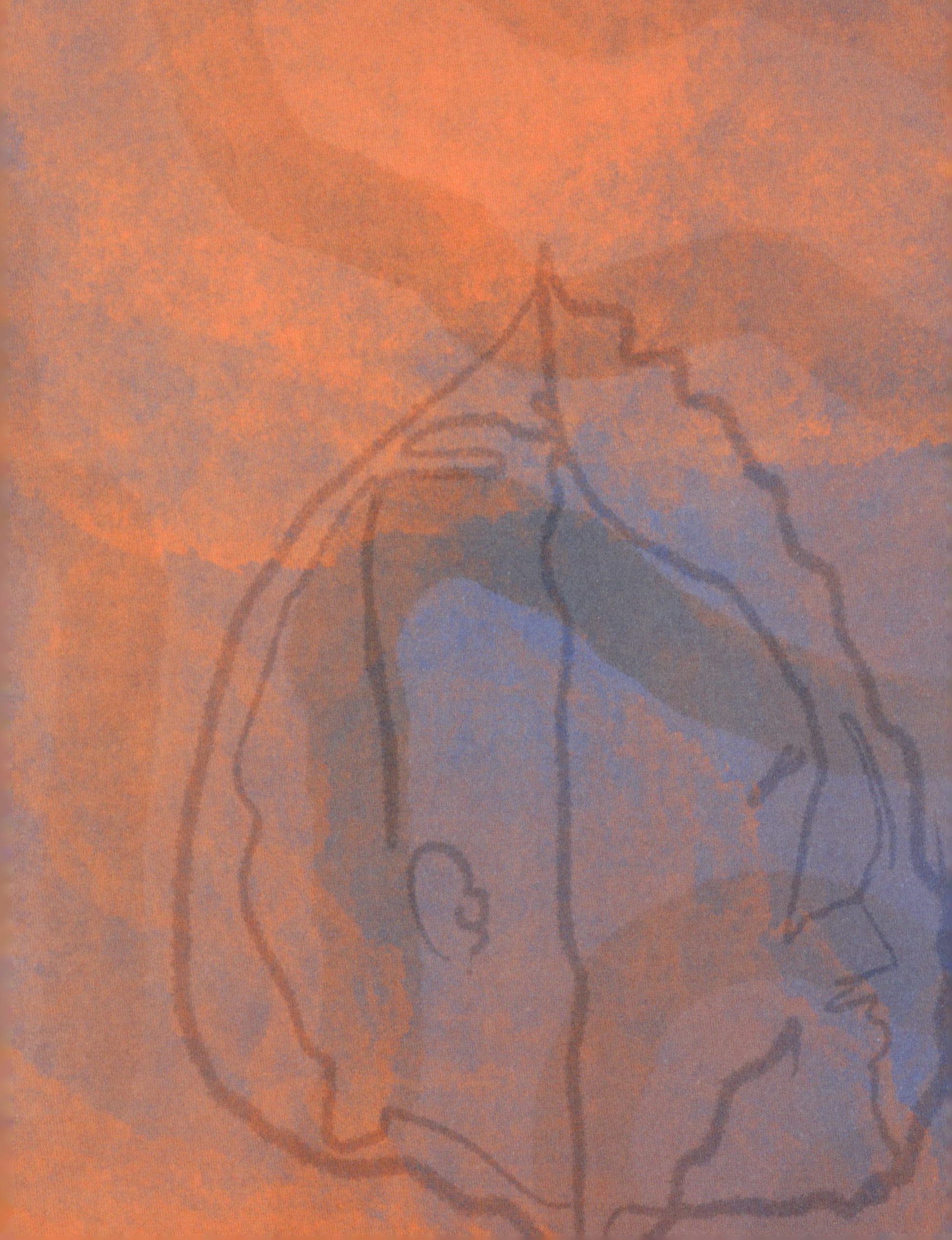

Dear Isaiah,

June 8, 2016, was a day that changed my life forever. I was lying on the couch with you on my chest, breathing you in, watching your little mannerisms while you slept. I felt the moment was perfect. But then the phone rang.

Some moments take hold in your brain and never let go. This was one of them. Your Aunty Nik called out of the blue to say that our beloved mother, your grandmother, Wendy, had passed away. I will always remember how I felt in that moment. It was as though all that was keeping me going had suddenly dissolved. I had only been speaking to her a couple of nights before, yarning about what had happened on the ABC's *Q&A* program. Now, this vivacious, loving, strong-willed, life of the party and adoring grandmother was gone. A connection to our culture, gone. She was only fifty-five years old, far too young to go.

You know the games we play together on your game machine? They are the same ones that as kids, we used to play together with Grandma. Grandma also loved her music, we used to listen to the Beatles, INXS, U2, Bruce Springsteen. We used to joke that we could hear Grandma Wendy before we saw her, because the music in her car was so loud. That is why we love listening to music at home now. She adored you and Ava. You were known as her little Grandbunnies. She would tell anyone and everyone about you kids.

The next month, organising her funeral, was a blur. I would not have been able to do it without your mother Hilda, Aunty Nikita, brother Benjamin, and the support of our many friends and family. The day was a beautiful celebration of Wendy's life, Isaiah. We listened to some of her favourite music during the service, and we were blessed to have Uncle Moogy Sumner perform a smoking ceremony on the day.

A few weeks later, on 25 July 2016, I watched the ABC's *Four Corners* program in horror. Australia was given an insight into the lives of young people who were incarcerated in the Northern Territory's Don Dale Youth Detention Centre. The horrific footage showed Aboriginal children between the ages of twelve and sixteen being beaten, stripped and held down; they were hooded and strapped to chairs; left in the heat and the cold; and tear-gassed by the guards of the facility. These were human rights violations. There has been no true justice for what they suffered.

A few days later I found out that one of the children was from Borroloola, a small Aboriginal community twelve hours drive from Darwin. Borroloola is our Country, my grandmother, your great-grandmother, was born there. We are Gudanji and Wambaya people.

The child could very well be related to us. He could be my nephew or my cousin. I was saddened and angry to see children treated this way. I thought of you, the challenges you will face in life as a young Aboriginal person – profiled for criminal intent because you are Blak – and the mistakes you may make, as we all tend to make as we find our way. Your mother and I will try to ensure that you and Ava are safe.

August 4 is National Children's Day for Aboriginal and Torres Strait Islander people. It should be a day to celebrate, to acknowledge that our children have a special belonging to this Country, and to strengthen pride in their cultural identity. Instead, this day in 2016 was marred by the publication of a political cartoon in *The Australian* newspaper. The cartoon, drawn by Bill Leak, showed a police officer bringing an Aboriginal child to what appears to be an Aboriginal father. The father, barefoot and with a beer in hand, makes a comment to the police officer as if to say he did not know the name of his own child.

That cartoon projected a negative stereotype – an incredibly negative stereotype. It said that Aboriginal men were drunks. It said that Aboriginal men did not know their children. It said that we do not care. In a single image, Leak had undermined my love for my children, belittled my relationship with my parents, and shifted the blame from the governments and the guards of Don Dale onto the victims' families. It was all based on a stereotype that represents no more than the minority. It was ignorant to why that minority may have social problems. To me, this was a racist depiction of our people and it enraged me.

At that point, the emotion was charged. The grief of losing Mum, the shock of the Don Dale abuse and now my rage at this cartoon converged into a perfect storm. It would have been so easy to act out in anger, son. But our people have been harbouring an angry fire in our bellies for 230 years. And although we have every right and cause to be angry, I think there comes a point when anger is not the right place to come from.

Isaiah, one thing I want you to take away from this is that people do not listen to you when you are angry. There is already too much anger in the world. I wanted to tell Bill Leak that I am a proud Aboriginal father. I wanted to say that I know both you and Ava. I wanted to say, 'Hey I don't mind a few beers, but I'm not a drunk.' And finally, I wanted to tell him, 'Bill, I do not fit your stereotype of an Aboriginal man, and nor do any of the Aboriginal men I know.' Bill Leak and the newspaper that published him were racist and wrong.

I turned the anger on its head and posted a simple image of you and Ava and myself to Twitter. I said simply that I am a proud Aboriginal dad. You both make me a proud Aboriginal dad! This image of us gave rise to #IndigenousDads on social media.

We spent that day with family, Aunty Faith was over from Perth. I didn't give that tweet another thought. It was a nice, sunny afternoon and we decided to put you and Ava in the pram and walk to the local pub. It was good catching up with Faith because we had not seen her for a while, and she wanted to spoil you kids. In the pub, you and I were focused on the football on the big TV.

Little did I know, this single tweet had ignited a social movement. When I looked at my phone, #IndigenousDads had spread like wildfire. Thousands of pictures were posted using the hashtag, photos of Aboriginal men and their children, of Aboriginal women and their fathers; politicians, sporting stars, actors and community activists all shared photos that countered the racist stereotype amplified by *The Australian*. Within forty-eight hours, these images overshadowed the distasteful cartoon that had catalysed their existence.

The offence this cartoon caused to both the Aboriginal community and their supporters was made obvious. In the aftermath of its publication, Leak's cartoon amassed over 700 complaints to the Australian Press Council. And yet, both Leak and the paper that employed him stood by the cartoon, denying all accusations of racism. The newspapers and conservative commentators used the term 'freedom of speech'. They said they were able to stand behind what was drawn without censorship, restraint or legal penalty.

Son, if you try to beat the media at their own game, you will never win. Even after 700 complaints, the National Press Council decided not to sanction the cartoonist or the newspaper. The National Press Council said the cartoon did not cause 'substantial offence, distress or prejudice'. But I say that Leak and *The Australian* and the Press Council were wrong. In the words of George Washington, 'Truth will ultimately prevail where there are pains taken to bring it to light.'

Because of the #IndigenousDads movement, I was asked to deliver a TEDx Talk on Kaurna land about the occasion. I was initially quite nervous, but at the same time I was excited at the opportunity to talk about how we were affected, and how social media provided a way to help drive social change.

In the months beforehand, I talked with the people who are closest to me as I formulated ideas for the speech. I watched speeches by famous people, such as Barack Obama, to help me understand oratory styles. Obama speaks quite slowly, and I learnt that this is an important way to get your message across. I practiced my speech for hours in front of the mirror and in front of your mother, who was vital to the fine tuning. I was nervous delivering that ten-minute oration, but I was prepared. Because I practiced, and because I had good advice from people I trusted, my TEDx Talk was a success. You know what, Isaiah, when I stepped on to the stage, I felt the presence of your Grandmother Wendy. She was watching over me. I believe she was there to help me succeed.

These are lessons I can pass on to you now, son. I feel that I delivered the speech well enough to move people, because despite people like Bill Leak and newspapers like

The Australian, I am proud of who I am. I practiced and worked hard to overcome a challenge, and I did it while accepting the support of those I trust. Your mum and I will always do our best to guide you, as you find your way through life.

One need only search #IndigenousDads on social media to learn that Bill Leak was wrong. Indigenous men can feel encouraged that social media can be a useful way to bypass the stereotype. It allows the people who are affected by an issue to join the conversation. And when their voices – millions of voices – come together, they are very powerful. Powerful enough to drive social change.

Our people, Gudanji and Wambaya, have been excluded for most of Australia's short existence but we have survived outside of the mainstream. We must always find new ways to be heard as we did with #IndigenousDads, and as we seek to do with the Uluṟu Statement from the Heart, which proposes the most powerful change possible – changing the Australian Constitution so it recognises our First Nations' voices.

Isaiah, Mum and I will teach you and Ava about our culture, our history, our family. You may hear ignorant views about your heritage from your teachers, from the media, from social media and sometimes, even your mates. We will equip and empower you to challenge their views in a respectful way. If your teachers say to you that Australia was founded in 1788, we empower you to say that our

'Truth telling allows a person, a people, a country to heal.'

people have been here for more than 60,000 years. If kids in the school yard talk about why so many Aboriginal and Torres Strait Islander people are locked up, we empower you to tell them that this is a direct result of policies that have occurred in the past. Son, this is called truth telling.

Truth telling allows a person, a people, a country to heal. Hearing this truth will be tough for some. They may feel ashamed when they hear the truth. You might have teachers or friends who say, 'I am not responsible.' You can say to them you are not asking them to blame themselves, but you are asking that they acknowledge that this is part of our country's shared history, and it is about time we all did something about it. We empower you to say this to the world.

Love from,

Your dad

JOHNNY LIDDLE

Arrernte/Luritja

To my dear sons, John, Daniel and Ryan, and my big grandson, Tyreece,

This letter is to you all as you reach different, but important, waypoints in your lives.

John, you are big and tough, and you aren't one to put up with nonsense. You don't talk much, but your actions are louder than your words. You work in road construction – hard yakka in the Central Australian bush. There're not too many Australians who would understand the physical work you do, the remoteness and the challenging isolation – not many in this country could handle it. You are thirty-nine now. You have been a good son to me and your mother, and we're proud that you are getting your life together. Your eleven-year-old daughter, who lives interstate now, is proud of you too. You may not realise it, but you are a good role model, both to your daughter and to your brothers.

Ryan, you're the youngest of my boys at thirty-three. You are pursuing your career in Sydney as a journalist. When we see you on TV, my heart overflows with pride. You look so slick, son. It's like you were always meant to be on the screen, doing important work, reporting on important things. What the TV audience won't know is that you are just as comfortable in the red dirt of our Central Australian home – on your Arrernte/Luritja Country.

Perhaps being in the big city makes coming home and going for a hunt all that more special. Like the other weekend when you came back. It was good to see you with your mates again – your mates who are also like my sons. You grew up with plenty of brothers who were not your blood – Blak and white. I think that makes you stronger. When we go out on Country, you and your brothers take on leadership roles, compete with each other, and learn from each other. None of you blokes are afraid to get your hands dirty chasing a kangaroo or knocking a killer. I can feel the pride you boys have in yourselves on the land, fending for yourselves and surviving. When I saw you behaving like that, it reminded me of when I was a young fella, chasing some excitement with mates. But I'll tell you more about me later.

And Daniel in the middle at thirty-six. Your milestone is reaching a crucial time in your own fatherhood journey. Your boy, Tyreece, is coming of age. You have set a good example for him, always working hard. And it has been hard – hard for you both. Being a FIFO worker, with your partner, a stepmother to your son, has great challenges. And COVID-19 these last twelve months has made it harder. Yet you have always provided and cared for Tyreece. And, our way, Tyreece has had, and will continue to have, all of us to guide him. Daniel, you've raised your son to be a fine young man who you can be proud of, as your family is of you both.

Tyreece, you are seventeen. I write this letter mostly for you. Your milestone of adulthood is coming along fast now. You have been wanting to leave home for a while – you're as eager as I was to make my own mark. But pause for a moment, now. Listen.

While I want you all to know I am proud of who you are, I also want you to know that I understand how life can be a challenge. The twists and turns we experience are impossible to plan for completely. It takes a lot of grit to cope sometimes. I want to help you find the determination to keep driving forward, and the best way I know how has always been to remember those who came before us.

If we were all home on Country, we would lay back in our swags, breathing the cool desert air into our lungs, and I'd tell you to look to the stars. Three generations staring into the sky together. I'd show you how the ancestors are watching us, with a twinkle in their eyes, and tell you what they teach us. For the sake of this letter, though, I will keep it much shorter than that. Let us look at the lessons I can teach you from the generations of Elders closest to us, starting with my father.

My father was stolen from his mum when he was around five or six years old. His mother was away, working just out of Alice Springs at Hamilton Downs Station. His father, a white man – a decent white man who looked after his Aboriginal kids – he couldn't stop him being taken either. It's the way it was in those days. Half-caste kids were a target.

My father rarely swore. He was a proper gentleman. And he rarely spoke about when he was taken away. On his deathbed, though, he recalled, 'The bastard had blue eyes.' I suppose he was talking about the policeman who stole him.

They took your grandfather when he was just a little boy to a place they called the Bungalow. I think 'Bungalow' was a slang word for the building – it was a big, fancy looking mission house. There were plenty of stolen kids who were sent there to be schooled – basically, to be assimilated and trained to be slaves. If you think about it, the Bungalow was a prison.

I have been to the Bungalow lots of times. It is in a national park now and I was a ranger. Whenever I went near that old, whitewashed stone building, it was like there was a smell about the area. I don't know if this is a good description, but I'm saying, the place smelt like sadness.

Before the Bungalow became a mission, it was originally one of the repeater stations for the overland telegraph. Then when technology moved on, it became a relay station for the telephone. In the mission, they had all the kids in the dormitories by night, and during the day, the kids were trained to work for the white man. They got a limited education, up to grade six. The boys were groomed to take on the roles of stockmen. The girls, as housekeepers and domestics.

I'm sure a lot of them suffered high levels of abuse and torment, but many kept their experiences to themselves throughout their lives. Some took what happened to them to an early grave, because their minds were tormented by the abuse. It was like they couldn't wake up from the nightmare of it all, and only the grog could numb the pain.

I attended a reunion around twenty years ago. It was at the Bungalow. The Stolen Generations Committee were doing some great work to reunite families and to organise reunions like this one – work that is still being done today. You can't imagine how badly families were torn apart.

The old people were so happy to see each other. They were old and frail, in their seventies and eighties. I could see it took a lot of energy from them, so many emotions, being in that place; but at the same time, it seemed to recharge them.

There were a lot of familiar names at that reunion. Familiar names because the kids and grandkids of these Elders had been champions in sport or in their careers. Families such as the Kruegers, champions at footy, and the Tilmouths and Furbers, who had done a lot of work for our mob. I talked to them and it was a great opportunity to learn about how they survived. I noticed that although they were bent with a hard physical life, despite all they had been through, on that day they stood tall. They told me stories with cheeky grins, like they were young again in that moment. It was a moving experience to meet them. All of them said they were happy to have been educated through the Stolen Generations process. It appeared that none of those great survivors was bitter about their treatment.

When my father was twelve years old, against his will he was apprenticed to a white station owner. It was the same for all the Bungalow kids. They were sent out to live and work in very harsh conditions, away from their families, if they knew who they were, and were forced to do the work of a grown-up.

My father was basically in a jail without bars. He could not leave the station without the permission of a white man. The stations owner and the Chief Protector controlled his every move.

As I said earlier, my father didn't swear often, but he described the station manager as a pig of a man. He must have been bad. They would have got floggings from them station whitefullas, and no doubt they weren't fed well. My old man never talked about getting paid. I am sure they were only on rations.

My dad did everything he could to get away from his tormentors. I remember seeing a letter he wrote. The writing was in pencil, on what looked like scrap paper he had scrounged. It was clearly written by a pre-teen with limited education. The letter was probably sent in secret, or he would get flogged.

It was written to the faceless bureaucrat in Darwin who controlled Blak kids' lives. In humble words, my dad requested he be moved to a nearby station where he knew he would be better treated. The bureaucrat in Darwin may as well have been an alien in another world. But Dad sent the letter and hoped for the wheels of justice to turn in his favour.

I do not know how or why, but the whitefulla in Darwin approved the transfer. My dad was pretty lucky, but he didn't rely on luck. He worked bloody hard to give me, and in turn, you fellas, a good life.

When my father got his freedom, he and my mother lived in an old shack. Mum, who you know as Nanna Bess, is still alive today, and she was one of five or six siblings. Nanna Bess grew up in the traditional way, but her life was altered by the barriers put up by the settlers around the place.

My mother's mother and father would travel up and down the waterways, such as the Finke River that goes right up to Hermannsburg and the Hugh River. Along the permanent waterholes, up and down. They travelled like a caravan, the families, herds of goats, a chook or two and donkeys, always followed by camp dogs – like greyhounds but big and well trained to hunt kangaroo, or marlu. Nanna said they lived on traditional food, such as marlu, and bush onion, or yarlke. It was the kids' job to make noise, and with the dogs, they would chase the kangaroos to where the men were ready with spears. It was a hard but fun way for them to live, but they were always in fear of the white men. The white men wanted the waterholes for their livestock and to them, our people were like pests.

My mum's mum was a real culture woman. She made sure Nanna Bess became a leader in our law. Your Nanna was stolen too and was taken to the Bungalow. She also recalls the brutal assimilation. She told me this story once about how her mum came to the Bungalow in the middle of the night and stole her back. We don't know much more about that old lady. She must have been an incredibly brave woman. We really should ask Mum more about her before it's too late.

My sons, be proud of who you are and where you have come from. I don't tell you about the hardships of your Elders to say that your lives are easy, but so you remember to never let your Elders' perspectives out of sight. They guide us. We are their legacy. The Liddle family has a long history in Central Australia, and we established a reputation for being hard working, innovative, ambitious, inclusive and knowledgeable. We were proud to be fierce advocates for human rights for our people, before it became fashionable. A bit like my long hair when I was a young bloke.

When I was the same age as my father was when he became a slave, at around twelve years old, I was just starting to smile at pretty girls while having fun annoying my teachers. We worked on the family cattle station that my father's white father had owned. It was a man's work at this age, during our school holidays, but for us it was enjoyable, as compared to working under a cruel white man. And we knew we would be going back to school for the easy life.

I hated school. I was myall – I was wild. I wanted to be free from the place because I had come from living with proper traditional people, speaking language and practicing culture. I only had a little bit of English. We walked around barefoot – just kids of the bush. Killed birds with a shanghai. Caught lizards to eat. Walked around learning about and exploring our Country. Having fun, riding a donkey, climbing trees. That's how it was.

As much as I hated school, our parents encouraged us to learn to read and write. They wanted us to learn so we could come back to help the family with what we learnt. My mum never learnt to read and write at the Bungalow. Still today, when we visit her, she always has a letter there for us to read. Illiteracy doesn't mean she isn't very wise. Life wasn't about reading and writing for them – it was about survival. Now, we must be educated to survive.

When I finished school at seventeen, I tried to get a job at a few places in Alice Springs. I didn't want to go bush at that age, there were temptations in town. I had to persevere to get a job because most employers looked me up and down before telling me they were not hiring. A few weeks later, though, I would see someone else working there. I suppose having long hair – which was frowned upon in them days – and being a bit of a show-off, didn't help my chances.

When I got a job, I still had to overcome racism. I wouldn't put up with it for long; if someone was being racist to me, I'd eventually tell them where to stick it and move on. I'd find another job, even if I was just digging holes to make a living. I called them jobs, Aboriginal jobs – where most of us worked.

The racism was bad, and it will affect you for the rest of your life. When I found my ideal workplace in Aboriginal health, I saw how racism affected men like us, especially during the 2007 Northern Territory National Emergency Response, or as most people know it, the Northern Territory Intervention.

The Prime Minister who made The Intervention was John Howard. Basically, it was his government portraying us Aboriginal men as molesters – ostracised as the doers of evil. They moved the army into our communities and put up signs banning pornography and alcohol. Most of our men didn't even know what pornography was. They saw it on the sign and asked what it was. Turns out that the government decided to do The Intervention based on lies.

All Aboriginal men felt guilty. I remember standing in Coles at the time of The Intervention. All these whitefullas were looking at me. I felt they were thinking I was a molester. Same day I saw a young Blak man holding his kid at the checkout, and I could see the way they looked at him, as if he was a molester. I could see it. I could feel it. They were thinking, You bastard, you are one of them, a molester.

I realised we needed to make things right. I wanted to have our own million-person march, like they did in America. I know there's not a million of us, but we organised a forum to talk about what The Intervention was doing to us.

The three-day forum was at Ross River, near Alice Springs. Almost three hundred Aboriginal and Torres Strait Islander men from across Australia gathered to discuss what was going on. Initially, the men were angry about what they were accused of.

I never did those things, they said. I never bashed my wife – but we are being blamed.

We had workshops to talk about our roles as men in our communities; what domestic violence is; how to be a good father. We were basically trying to build our men up. At the end of the forum, we agreed on a public statement pledging that we will not be silent about violence against women. Pledging our care and respect for Aboriginal women. We signed it, and politicians, bureaucrats and women came to receive the pledge.

That was an emotional and historic day. It was one of my proudest moments.

My sons, sometimes history is written by the ignorant and the eager whilst the people who have lived the history are not considered or consulted. This letter has been hard for me to write. It's difficult for me to do, but let's think of this as the start of a yarn – a yarn we can continue around the campfire when we are all back home. The lesson now

‘Learn from my example and the example of your Elders. Respect women – treat them with love and respect.’

is, learn from my example and the example of your Elders. Respect women – treat them with love and respect. We all come from a woman somewhere.

Lastly my boys, let us always respect and thank our old people for taking the brunt of the despair, suffering and mental and physical abuse, and surviving. And remember that before them, before the white man ever came, we lived a peaceful and happy existence. An existence that with perseverance, hard work, love and respect for each other, we can recreate.

Your dad and pop,

Johnny Liddle

Joe Williams

Wiradjuri, Wolgalu on Wiradjuri land

My Long Son,

I call you that, son, not because of how tall you are compared with me, but because of your long arms and legs.

I will start this letter by letting you know I love you! These are the three most important words anyone can say to someone, especially to their own son. For me, it means so much to tell you how I feel about you. I believe it is also important to say the less obvious things because that is where some of life's greatest lessons can be learnt.

As you know, mate, most of my life has been about sport. I was lucky enough to play sport as my job for years, first as an NRL player and then as a professional boxer. Watching your Pop play on TV and then your Uncle Mike play locally, I wanted to be like them – they were tough, skilful and proud. I always wanted to be a footy player.

Some people might think that being a professional sportsman was cool, or that I was so lucky. That is true – I am extremely lucky to have achieved many of my personal goals, from playing in the NRL for the South Sydney Rabbitohs to winning titles as a boxer. These achievements didn't come without life-threatening challenges, though; challenges I survived. While I was a little lost for a few years, I found my way back onto the path through my connection to Country, and the values I was taught in my childhood. I was lucky to have had a good connection to Country, and a childhood where I was loved.

Your Nin (Nan), a Wiradjuri woman, and Pop, who is Wolgalu, did everything they could for me, the best way they knew how. Their kids, your aunties and uncles and I, we didn't have it flash. There wasn't much money around and we didn't have many material things, but instead our parents taught us life lessons and values. We learnt about the importance of showing love, care and respect for others, and especially the Elders. In line with our First Nations culture, we learnt that doing more for others than what you do for yourself is the key to life.

Nin and Pop taught us these lessons through their example. Whenever our many cousins came to town, they'd always stay at our house. We fed them and gave them our beds, even when we didn't have much for ourselves. Nin and Pop were very generous, and they passed these values on to us.

While I have had some amazing experiences as a sportsperson, I will always say to anyone who will listen: 'My sporting career has been a blessing, but my greatest achievement is being a dad to five of the best kids any parent could wish for.'

You are the oldest of all my kids, and when I first laid eyes on you, I burst into tears. They were tears of sheer joy and absolute love and pride. I thought, How on earth could I have played a part in producing someone so beautiful and perfect? In fact, while writing this and considering how proud I was of you when you were growing up and my pride in the young man you are today, I am in tears again.

From the moment you were born, I knew you would be a fighter, a strong Larrakia–Wiradjuri-Wolgalu young baabin (baby), who would one day grow into a strong, resilient man.

You might ask how I could be so sure about this when you were a little baby.

Well, mate, when you were only two weeks' old and diagnosed with Supraventricular tachycardia (SVT), a heart condition that saw your heart beating at around 300+ beats per minute, I just knew that your heart was strong. I knew you would be able to withstand the toughest adversities.

In the early days, when you started to crawl and move yourself around, you were so quiet and so quick. Your mum and I would often panic when we didn't know where you were, and we'd frantically search around in our small unit. Finally, we'd find you entertaining yourself, all alone, without a care in the world.

While I was preparing for the 2005 season with the South Sydney Rabbitohs, a prominent east coast news outlet wanted to take a photo of you and me. So, that week, when you were only a couple of weeks' old, your face was splashed across the front page of a major national newspaper. I remember saying to your mum, 'There are leading stories about all kinds of dramas going on throughout the world, and here we are, a pic of our son and me going into the homes of people across Australia.'

When your sister came along, even though you were still a baby yourself really, you already knew to be gentle. That gentle, soft and caring touch has been a part of you since birth – it is in your nature still today.

You are my oldest child and a leader for your younger brothers and sisters. I want to help you to avoid repeating some of my behaviours when I was a young man. I also want you to understand that our feelings and behaviours are always a reflection of what is happening in our lives and what has happened in the lives of those who came before us. We carry the trauma that has been handed down for many generations due the ongoing impact of colonisation.

I had a deep conversation with your Pop recently, about the traumas he lived through, and he told me how he grew up in a tough time for Blackfellas. He was raised in a Catholic missionary community where people lived with the continual pressure to adapt to a new, assimilated way of life. They lived with constant scrutiny from government workers, who dutifully tried to take away our culture, and if you didn't do as they demanded, they could take your children away. In the Bringing Them Home Report, they say at least 100,000 children were stolen. This is what is known as the Stolen Generations.

Pop's dad, your great-grandfather, died when Pop was just nine, and Pop had already lost a sister. Your great-grandfather's death put all sorts of pressure on the family, mostly on your great-grandmother, Nan Ollie, who we are lucky to still have with us. Nan Ollie is an incredibly resilient woman. She raised all of her eleven kids pretty much on her own. I can't imagine how hard that would have been, especially while facing the threats and prejudice that our colour and heritage brought against her and her family. Without a doubt, they suffered physical, emotional and spiritual pain – pain that caused traumas which have been passed on to us.

In sport, anyone would think I was successful, but I was having a constant battle with an enemy within. To put a bandaid on my feelings, I partied and drank alcohol. These were hard times that led to the separation of our family when you were about five years old. I wrote about this struggle and of those times in my book, Defying the Enemy Within.

Getting sober was the key to my recovery, but once I took the alcohol out of my system, the noise in my head became louder. It was like I was using alcohol as a bandaid for the pain I was going through mentally and emotionally. If I took the bandaid off, the pain got worse

That was a tough period for all of us. Your mum and I separated, and you were forced to grow up before your time. For that, mate, I am so sorry. I don't think I considered the impact it had on you, your sister, or your mum. And that was really selfish of me.

Talking and writing about my challenges, being honest

'Talking and writing about my challenges, being honest with myself and everyone around me, has been difficult, but also healing.'

with myself and everyone around me, has been difficult, but also healing. The most important lesson I can teach you is that the greatest healing comes from being honest with yourself and others and connecting to our culture and Country. The being honest part can be confronting, it our culture and connection that keep us grounded.

People think our culture is just beautiful dances and artworks, but culture is also about how we practice our values – how we treat each other. For more than sixty millennia, we have been a sharing, communal people. Nin and Pop continued this with their example of unselfishly looking after others.

It is our connections with each other and our land that kept us well before the Europeans came. They tried to separate us from our culture and lands but we survived, and we still march for our land rights.

Connecting to Country is harder today. We are trying to navigate life in two worlds, training and working in our careers and, for many of us, living away from our Country. It is important that despite these difficulties, we continue our cultural practices and live with the values. It is important that we as First Nations people continue to come together to connect in the old ways – through celebration, through ceremony and the many, various expressions of who we are. This is why I always do my best to take you out on Country – to keep you connected, to keep you healthy, spiritually, mentally and emotionally.

'It is important … we continue our cultural practices, and live with the values – love, care, respect, humility and compassion.'

My journey has been confronting yet empowering, and it's a continual journey. Healing is an ongoing process. I don't expect that you will be perfect, son, or that I will no longer make mistakes; we will always make mistakes. Mark my words, there will be challenging times. They will come throughout your life, in your relationships, in your sport and in your career.

You have your own dreams and goals. Whatever they may be, choose to achieve them with the values I write about in this letter – love, care, respect, humility and compassion. Walk tall, but don't ever think it is shameful to show vulnerability, son. There is enormous strength in being vulnerable. By being comfortable in sharing your vulnerabilities, you'll grow and learn how to be a better man.

I am so proud of the love and leadership you give your brothers and sisters. Although living in different households, they idolise their big brother, and you have never once showed them anything but love. Continue to lead by example. Make sure you always love and look after your mum and respect all women. You come from a mother, and when you die you will return to Mother Earth.

Finally – love – love is the key to growth in everyone's heart. Keep loving, mate. Love with everything you have. The world needs less hate, and more love!

I'm proud of you, and I love you more than you will ever know.

Dad xox

Listen now bub

Hey, my bub,

Be proud of who you are

the continuation – the survival

of the oldest continuing culture on Earth

This is your land
Those are your stars
These are your waters
The beaches
The forests
The mountains
The bush
The jungles
The deserts
The winds and the seas

We are older than Europe – and intact

As their kingdoms crumbled
We were at peace – for millennia

They tried to conquer nature
We see it as part of ourselves

We are a continuation – survivors

Be proud of who you are

Hey, my bub.

DANIEL JAMES

Yorta Yorta, Gunaikurnai

Dear Dad,

You lived a textured life. One full of colour and movement. A life dedicated to family, friends and your brothers in arms in the Army. A life largely without sickness, except towards the end. You were incredibly healthy.

The last time I spoke to you it was late in the night, or at least it seemed late. At moments like that one, time slows down. Memories seemed so fleeting; patches and flashes of emotion crashed into my thoughts when least expected, least convenient. Probably like the way I used to storm into your room as a toddler, while you were resting after a long week on the road for work.

The conversation was brief, it had to be. You could barely breathe. 'I'm not in pain, Dan, I'm just…it's frustrating,' you husked down the line.

We were trying to organise for Ethan and Hayley to see their Pop one last time. It was Monday night; they couldn't get to you in Echuca until Wednesday. 'Wednesdee?' I could hear you doing the sums in your head, like you were calculating how many jerry cans you would need to make it to Horsham, and what time you would need to hit the road. Except this time, you were figuring out whether you'd still be around to tell them how much you loved them. You knew then you'd run out of breath.

Although you all loved each other, you needed to say it, and they needed to hear it. Neither eventuated. You were gone early the next morning. The sky was so red that morning, sailor's warning.

You were the first generation off the mission, one step removed from the collective memory of your Elders; one of the many of your mob who were trying to make their way through the cracks in society where opportunity sometimes bloomed, like dandelions in a footpath. For you, that dandelion was the Army. An army that went to Vietnam.

You never told us what it was like to be a Blak man in a racist organisation during a racist time, where you were a pariah in an army of pariahs. Perhaps your silence was a result of the opposition to the war itself. Maybe you thought the details would be boring to us kids. Maybe what you lived through was far too painful to recount. It was a photo that gave me a glimpse into your pain. Adorning the fridge for many years was a platoon intake photo. Among other boys, expected to be men, was twenty-one year-old you. The commanding officer's face was scribbled out with pen so violently it left a hole in the photo. I never asked you about it, I didn't have to.

When you passed away, I was affected in ways I never expected. I suddenly felt alone in the world. After a Tigers' win or loss, usually a loss, I felt like the phone was broken. Surely you'd ring.

One of life's oddities, of course, is that I am far from alone in experiencing that sense of abandonment. Almost everyone who loses a parent feels this way. Every loss is unique. Every episode of grief is its own expensive cocktail of memories, sorrow, anger and hurt. No two are the same. That's why grief is important, it has to play its own course, there's so much to let out, to let go. Writing this letter is part of that process.

Maybe you could've written to Nanny James as I am writing to you. You suffered badly when we lost her. Your grief played itself out in a myriad of ways over the rest of your life. Some too personal for me to write about here. I like to think I was there for you in those moments, but I wasn't. Mum had left, us kids had grown up and gone. I'm sorry you went through those times alone.

I wonder if your greatest companion was the road. You worked on the road as a Telecom linesman for decades. Your knowledge of the Hume Highway was second to none. Up and down you went, as a driver, a passenger, and in your younger days, as a hitchhiker. You walked your Country, made your own songlines, despite them never being handed down to you.

It makes me think about how our connection to Country doesn't need to be written. Nor does it need to be handed down in oral history, as it would have if we weren't disrupted by colonisation and an ongoing lack of recognition. We feel that connection. And if we can feel it, we can strengthen it, back to how it was. You passed that on to me. I wonder if you knew.

‘Our connection to Country doesn’t need to be written … we feel that connection.’

You lived the largest part of your life moving along the flanks of the Hume Highway. Between Wangaratta, Benalla and Euroa for forty-five of your sixty-five years. A truck's air brakes rumbling in the night were the A and B sides to the soundtrack of your life. You were blue collar through and through.

When I was a kid, I went on a drive with you to Melbourne. We were listening to the radio, and the bloke on the radio mentioned something about working with colleagues. You rolled your eyes and said, 'Colleagues! What a tool.' This attitude had grown from the indignity you'd experienced together with your suspicion of white-collar workers generally, I suppose. I often wondered what you thought I looked like in my suit and tie when you picked me up at Euroa station.

Now I think about it, you had a unique relationship with the English language. And you made sure I knew it. The first time was when I foolishly referred to the MCG as the G. 'What?' you barked. 'It's the MCG, not the "G". Where did that come from?'

The other time, and I should have known better, was when I said 'Nam' instead of 'Vietnam'.

'What's this Nam shit? It's Vietnam. Nam is a Yank thing,' you advised unequivocally. Fair enough too. After all, you did have 'Vietnam' tattooed on your arm. If you had just had 'Nam', I would have had means of recourse. You were pretty passionate about protecting Australian English from Americanisation. You didn't like me saying 'guys'. It had to be 'blokes'. This probably stemmed from an in-depth conversation we had when I was about four. I was trying to convince you that I was, in truth, an American. All the shows on television were American. All the music I heard was American, especially Kiss, which I had a particular affinity with, I'm told. Maybe it was that conversation that set you on the warpath against American slang. Yeah, you were a really passionate guy.

But back to the road. There wasn't enough money to send me to school camps, so one year it was decided I would go on the road with you to work for the week. I was disappointed not to go on camp, of course. I only ever went on one camp during my whole time at school. I knew I was missing out. Going away and spending twenty-four hours a day with your school mates built a new type of connection. Now I look back on it, I can see that the opportunity to go away with you for that week was probably the best week of my childhood.

On one trip, we had to pick up the rest of the work crew, all four of them, via West Footscray from Euroa. This meant we had to go via Bairnsdale to reach our ultimate destination, Omeo. It was going to be a long journey, that's for sure, but the old Ford Falcon, or the 'Scud' as you had christened it, was more than up to the task. Its odometer had stopped clicking over at the 200,000-kilometre mark. We'll never know how many ks you two did together. That day it felt we did all 200,000 of them in one go.

When I think of the yellow body, grey bonnet and green driver's side door of that car, my overwhelming memory is of the scent of tobacco and Old Spice. I rarely come across that scent anymore. Times have changed. On the few occasions that I have, it took me right back to riding shotgun with you on early mornings and late afternoons on the Hume, with Charley Pride playing on the tape deck. Charley's gone now too. I hope you can get tickets.

What about that time on the way to Omeo, when we had two tyre blowouts west of Bairnsdale on your mother's Country, Gunaikurnai Country? You had to hitch your way into town to replace the spare tire after the second blowout. I guess having about 500-odd kilos of unshaven humanity in the Scud would test the wall of any tire after a while.

We had broken down just the other side of Stratford, where your Nan Alice was born and where she was the victim of a heinous crime – raped by white men. A trauma that fractured her life, causing more traumas. You were never told. You knew she was strong, tough as nails, had a mouth like a trooper. You knew she was a bootlegger in the slums of Fitzroy in the 1930s. But you didn't know the burden she carried. The wounds she carried. She hid them from you, so you wouldn't grow up angrier than you had to.

Despite the inauspicious start that week, you worked hard, and you were playful and relaxed. You showed me the back country around Omeo, about as remote as you can get in Victoria. Your wisecracking sense of humour was on full display, a trait I seem to have inherited. You were kind, you were generous, and you were my hero. You still are.

I often think about the searing summer temperatures in the Commission house we lived in in Benalla. We were lucky the cool waters of Broken River, so refreshing at dusk, we were only a short walk away. Those waters mended everyone's frayed edges.

You wouldn't have known this, Dad, but Benalla or Benwhalla (Big Water), as the local Waveroo people called it, was a meeting place for at least three tribes, the Bangerang, Taungurong and the Waveroo. You may have seen the plaque in Mair Street alluding to it being a scared site or some such to the local Aboriginal people. But that's as close as you would have got to any anthropological lesson about your forbears. That and the other plaque erected a hundred years after the death of a woman believed to be the last member of the Bangerang, Mary Jane Milewa, who died on 10 October 1888. You had long left Benalla by the time that memorial was set in stone.

What chance did you have to learn about the traditional way of life, when those who could have told you were wiped out at least three generations before you were born?

You inherited the traditions of the modern Koori: street smarts and a willingness to fight. You ended up in the lock-up so many times during your formative years, I find it amazing you never went to prison. You said people thought you had a chip on your shoulder, I think it was the other way around. The tension, the atmosphere of some of those small towns back then that would fill you with anxiety – the racism. We know who had those chips.

Your politics never changed, a union man through and through, voting Labor all your life. The alternative… well there was no alternative in your mind. Your views influenced mine as a kid, but my own understanding of the meaning of politics was truly galvanised during the early nineties, when I was a boy.

Living in a small town, a sheep farming community famous for Wool Week, soon after the High Court's Mabo decision that ended the fiction of terra nullius, was tough for us Koori mob down south. The racism we copped in the pubs, streets, football grounds and at school was aggravated by the truth being found in the highest court in Australia. The dogs were off their chains. My life was made hard by pumpkin-headed kids who were fed lies by their parents who, in turn, were told to fear us by opportunistic conservative politicians. It saturated everything – relationships, conversations and passing glances everywhere we went. White people thought that Blak people like us were coming to take their land – I wonder what that feels like...

You dubbed the collective mindset of those times as Small-Town Syndrome (STS). Very apt. It's just a pity STS is as much a diagnosis for the broader population. Dad, you can probably see from up in the stars with Nan that, in 2021, STS is firmly ingrained in the country you fought for. It's a pity you're not here to teach us anymore.

The mashing and thrashing around Mabo, Native Title and Wik continued in earnest for nearly five years. In that time, I gained a very clear idea of what I thought the world should look like, compared to how it was. Did those years give me a chip on my shoulder? No. They just affected my posture.

Your example during those times, your principled stance in the face of overwhelming opposition and ignorance, was perhaps the greatest life lesson you bestowed on me. You were fierce in your defense of your heritage and about what was right and what was wrong. Yet you never lost your sense of humour.

Here's that extract from the *Euroa Gazette* circa 1993, when you made it to the news at the height of Mabo and the Native Title debate.

MABO – MAYBE

There was a real verbal stoush at the entrance gate before our last home match against Mooroopna. The very popular Billy James – who is always willing to remind friends that he is very proud of his Aboriginal heritage – refused to pay his five bucks. Billy claimed it was a sacred site – and the land belonged to him anyway.

'You were fierce in your defense of your heritage and about what was right and what was wrong.'

The resultant conversation can't be recorded in your family newspaper. To cut a long story short Billy finally paid – under sufferance.

I read it out as part of your eulogy back in Euroa. It got a laugh then; it makes me smile still.

We learnt a lot about each other in your last years. I say last years and not latter years because the ages from sixty-two to sixty-five don't seem particularly late to me; they seem too early.

By the time I came back to spend time with you, you were the last Blackfulla in town. You had got your final tattoo by then, a small Koori flag across your chest. Somehow the sun was off center, probably because your heart was so big that it had its own center of gravity.

By this stage of your life and of our relationship, there was no longer any sugar coating of aspects of your history and the way you were feeling about the world and your place in it. There were truths told that were once untold. Feelings expressed that had once been repressed. And a quiet realisation there was more to look back on than to look forward to.

At home in your last years, you would sit staring across the corrugated-iron rooftop of your neighbour's home, watching the tall ghost gum changing colour and form in the afternoon light. It was mesmerising, the last of its ghostly glow disappearing at dusk. I wonder how many of your thoughts, feelings and regrets are caught in that majestic tree's foliage, fed from the waters of Seven Creeks nearby. If I think of a physical and spiritual manifestation of you now, it is that tree, by that creek.

It's the way these things happen.

You quietly told me once, 'It takes ten years to get over the death of a parent.' If that's the case, it's going to be a long three years.

Love,

Daniel

TIM SCULTHORPE

palawa

Dear Nico, ya malangina mina,

nika milaythina palawa, milaythina mana, palawa takara milaythina nara-mapali-ta, palawa mulaka, palawa kanaplila, palawa krakapaka milaythina nara-mapali-ta, waranta tunapri tunapri palawa.

This is our language, palawa kani, keeping our Elders and our Country close, like a thread that connects us through every word we speak. Hold on to that thread, so you will never get lost.

It's important to know where we come from so we can understand where we are going. It is our responsibility to keep our culture alive to guide the generations to come. Without our ancestors' struggle to survive, we would not be here today, and we must acknowledge them. In fact, this is why we acknowledge Country every night before bed, it is a new tradition for our family, and I want you to uphold it.

Your great-great-grandma, Fanny Smith, is one of the reasons why our language, palawa kani, exists today. In 1899 and 1903, she was recorded singing in palawa, and she was the only person to record a song in a Tasmanian Aboriginal language. These recordings provided your aunties, Grandad and our community with the opportunity to revive our language.

Even though I only know a handful of words of palawa kani, I have spoken it to you since you were in the womb and I continue to sing it to you each night. Perhaps

'Without our ancestors' struggle to survive, we would not be here today, and we must acknowledge them.'

Grandma Smith had a better singing voice than me. She certainly was an exceptional woman; she was one of the few palawa people who succeeded in convincing the authorities to give some of her land back. Grandma Smith had influence because she was the heart of the community, and of her kitchen, the heart of her home. She'd welcome guests with love and always have food for them to share.

Grandma Smith's husband was William Smith, an English sawyer and ex-convict. Their son Frederick was known for throwing the best parties in the Rivulet, his parties even made the papers in the Hobart *Mercury*.

Your Pop on my mother's side, Charles William (Bill) Evans, came from a family of entrepreneurs who started the Evans Store in Queenstown when the Mt Lyell copper mine opened in the nineteenth century. He expanded and modernised the business, adding a new building to include a supermarket and general store, selling everything you could think of. The store is still operated by the Evans family today.

One day, you'll hear more stories about Grandma Smith, about our old people and about your mother and me working towards the recognition of Aboriginal food in lutruwita (Tasmania). Grandma Smith's ability to survive and thrive, while keeping our culture alive, has set us in good stead.

My grandfather, your great-grandfather, Ray Sculthorpe, owned a farm, had a football grandstand named after him, loved to tell me a story about fighting colossal squids, all while raising your aunties and grandfather. He even survived being run over by a tractor. His success had much to do with his skills, work ethic and determination to achieve what he believed in, with a little bit of luck in the mix.

Grandad Ray fought in World War Two in Borneo and was lucky to survive. His section sergeant was killed in action and Ray was promoted in the field to lance corporal. Their mission was to protect or take control of a particular hill. Due to a misunderstanding, he took his men up the wrong hill; the sergeant who took a different section up the correct hill was shot and killed as he reached the top.

After World War Two, unlike many other Aboriginal soldiers, Grandad Ray was offered some land in north-west Tasmania to become a dairy farmer, as part of the Soldier Settlement Scheme. He declined this offer as it was not what he had applied for; the bureaucrats thought they knew what was best for Grandad. He wanted to start his own farm on the rivulet where he grew up, right next to where Grandma Smith had her land. What was most important to Grandfather Ray was his family, his community and his place in it. To follow his dream he needed to buy some land, but no bank would lend him money. In the end he was financed by the seller, his cousin Mr Miller, who had faith in his ability to repay.

Within a few years, your Grandfather Ray had turned his farm into an apple orchard. During the General Strike of 1953 in London, there were some issues with transporting apples from Australia to London. Grandfather Ray's harvest was later in the year and he decided to keep the apples on his trees longer, to take a gamble that the strike would be over. He put his Delicious apples on the ship *Timaroo Star*, and they arrived in London as the strike was coming to an end. The apples on every other vessel had spoiled. Your Great-Grandad was able to sell all his apples at a premium and pay off his debt within five years. This entrepreneurial spirit, coupled with luck, seems to run in the family.

My father, Roger Raymond Sculthorpe, taught me an important yet simple lesson about fatherhood, 'Be the fun one and keep them alive.' I hope you will come to know him well, he has always been there for me, always encouraged me to do what I want to do and be who I want to be. As the saying goes, he kept his kids alive.

Your Great-Grandad and Grandad are Aboriginal men, like you and me. Our people face major challenges, many of which stem from a lack of recognition of our culture and political rights as First Nations people. For a long time, we were told there were no more Tasmanian Aboriginal people left after the death of palawa woman Truganini, who died in 1876. It is true that the invaders and then the settlers drove our mob to the borders of extinction, but we are still here. It was hard being told we did not exist. But because of our people's stoic activism, more Australians than ever before have come to know the truth about our history and legacy. I hope that you will grow up in a fair and just world, a more understanding world, where you will not have to deal with the same ignorance.

One day you will wonder what being Aboriginal means to you. You might look at your reflection and wonder about the colour of your skin. I have always known I am Aboriginal. I have wished my skin were darker so I could feel like I belonged. This is why you make me enormously proud when we read the book *Our Home, Our Heartbeat* by Adam Briggs, and you high-five the page that states we are all different colours. You will learn it is not the colour of our skin that defines our Aboriginality, it is our ancestry, practice of culture and beliefs.

I feel privileged to be part of this family, to be part of the palawa mob, and to have this opportunity to pass it on to you, my son.

Having you has made me reflect on what kind of dad I want to be. As I write, I am watching you sleep, wondering what I can do, which lessons I can take from my life to help you and which of my mistakes I could tell you about, so I might save you the trouble of making the same mistakes yourself.

The first and most important advice I will give is that if you believe in something, go for it. Much like your Great-Grandad did when buying his land and turning down the

Soldier Settlement deal, or waiting for the right time to sell his apples.

We, as your parents, are here to guide you through this journey, but you must trust your instincts. I believe these instincts can be our Elders talking to you. You will hear them when you are ready to listen.

They spoke to me when I needed them the most. It was before you were born and when we were first considering starting our own business. I was with your Uncle Andry and cousins Marley, Asher and Penelope on a cultural camp trip. It was a milestone moment for us all as it was one of the first times in hundreds of years that we had permission to do a cultural burn, as our ancestors did.

As the day was coming to an end, we were finishing the final burn and Linton Burgess, a palawa dancer and cultural educator, ochred up and started dancing with the flames. When the fire had nearly died, the old people flared it up again for one last dance, and in that moment, I felt a renewed connection to Country – I heard Country calling on me to do more for my palawa community.

It is with that in mind and heart that we started a business against all odds: palawa kipli. It means Tasmanian Aboriginal food. I learnt a lot during this process and so many of those learnings I want to pass on to you.

When we first thought of palawa kipli I did not have the support of our family, your grandfather and uncles had some doubts about the idea and thought we were crazy. They were against it from a supportive perspective, wondering why I would leave a high paying corporate job that had me travelling the world to start one in food, with which we had limited experience. Despite their misgivings, they did save us on many occasions when we started the business, lending a helping hand when we needed it. You will get to know us, your family. We like excitement. You will learn one day that people look at life through different lenses shaped by their own experiences. I hope we will give you the tools to shape your own.

Now, do not get jealous if I tell you that palawa kipli was our first child – a brainchild. Your mum is Mexican of Spanish and Indigenous heritage. Her great-grandfather was well known because he had fought to preserve his Indigenous language, Nahuatl, and enjoyed telling his grandchildren stories of the greatness of Tenochtitlan, an ancient city near Mexico City. Your mum is an amazing woman. She is incredibly beautiful and is equally smart, and she has a strong heart. Your mum is passionate about the connection between culture and sustainability. And palawa kipli has succeeded because we learnt from Grandma Smith that it is good and wise to offer everyone a seat at our table.

We were starting a business and a family at the same time; it wasn't easy, but somehow, we were in the right place at the right moment, and we found kind people along the way. Remember to surround yourself with people who will bring you up rather than bring you down, and always be narakupa (kind).

The business was a quick success, making every major news outlet in Tasmania and some publications on the 'mainland', including the *Sydney Morning Herald.* We created this business with a focus on Aboriginal food, but we added a modern twist and homage to your mum's culture too. One dish in particular is the best combination of our cultures: the Bush Tuck-O. It's a Mexican-inspired tortilla infused with wattle seed and topped with bush-tucker ingredients, such as payathanima (wallaby) and pickled kunnigong (pig face). This was the single best mix of our cultures until you were born.

You arrived just in time for NAIDOC Week. It was the busiest time at palawa kipli. We were beginning to realise there was quite a risk trying to raise a baby without a stable income, but fate seemed to shine our way. An opportunity arose on Gadigal land in Sydney. The first not-for-profit Aboriginal tourism marketplace, Welcome to Country, was launching and they needed a Head of Marketing. Your Uncle AJ introduced me to the CEO.

After applying for the position, Welcome to Country flew us over for an interview. Two hours later we were sitting having lunch and I was offered the job. I took it because I have learnt a lot about our culture but not enough about other mobs' cultures. I wanted the opportunity to learn more. My life mission would remain the same

– to educate people about Aboriginal culture for a more sustainable future – but now, instead of running a food business in Tasmania, I have the chance to do it on a national scale and in a field I have extensive experience in. Your mother and I quickly packed up our stuff and worked closely with your Aunty June so she could become the custodian of palawa kipli while we figured out what we were doing. The Tasmanian Aboriginal Centre (TAC) saw the benefits palawa kipli brought to the community and the potential it had as a training ground for palawa youth, teaching them about cooking and also about culture, so they took over palawa kipli. To this day, I could not be prouder than when I see palawa youth being empowered and employed.

Son, you introduced me to a new kind of love that I could never have imagined. You make me want to be a better man. A better man so you can grow into a better man again. And by man, I do not mean the stereotypical man that I once was. We are lucky to live in a time when gender roles are pushed aside, when your mum and I can be a team, when I can see you enjoying a meal that I cooked for you, when I can stay at home and look after you, when I can tell you how I feel, so you will never go through anything alone, in fear of expressing your feelings.

I will always strive to be here for you, and I will always love you. Even if something were to happen to me, I will be watching over you, because when we palawa die, we are returned to the land to continue our circle of existence. To find me, you need only look to the stars, the skies and the trees. I want you to make your own mistakes and take your own risks, like I have. I want you to be proud of everything you are, the first palawa Mexican.

For your first birthday, we dressed you up as the world's first Aboriginal astronaut. It might have seemed silly, but that is our wish for you, to dream to be whatever you want out there in the universe.

Love from,

Dad

Many words in this essay are in palawa kani, the language of Tasmanian Aborigines, with thanks to the Tasmanian Aboriginal Centre. All words in palawa kani are written in lowercase.

A child's path

Provide the means for your children to illuminate their own paths, rather than have them mimic your shadows.

Listening is a language

Still, child, listen

There

Feel

See

Freely be

Pause

The ancestors are smiling

The old ones are guiding

Because you listen.

Dato's final breath

The son, how he cried
as dusk reached Dad's eyes
where daylight once was
and the dawn seemed so long ago.
He beckoned him close
with whispering breath
last vestige of knowledge bestowed.

You will find me, my son,
where waves massage memory
and the moon
is reflected on the sand.
With the ancestors above
impressing their love
upon me, upon you, and our land.

THOMAS MAYO

Zenadth Kes

Dear Dad,

When I announced I would become a writer, you said you wouldn't read my books. I wasn't hurt. Instead, I was emboldened.

You have always demanded that I mustn't talk about you to anyone – how you have managed to survive and provide. But here, in this letter, Dad, your modesty will be outdone by my pride.

And why shouldn't a son be proud of his father? You have overcome so much.

You came from Thursday Island in apartheid Queensland as a young man with nothing. You built a home with your own hands, even though you didn't have any qualifications as a builder. You and Mum did this on one meagre income, using aptitude, commitment and ultimately, your love for your children.

You taught me to hunt and fish on the reefs, and to cook as Torres Strait Islander men do. You taught me good values and discipline. You taught me to always work hard.

I have learnt that although your quick temper felt harsh, from your perspective, being hard on me was necessary. You were preparing me for a world that would not love me like you do. You figured that a foot up the backside at home was better than me putting a foot wrong outside, where making a poor decision could land me in prison, or perhaps six foot under the ground.

'You were preparing me for a world that would not love me like you do.'

I have idolised you and, with age, I have learnt to follow where you shine the light, without walking in your shadows. I am educated, patient and generous because of you. I am imperfect like you. And with as many of your lessons as I could gather, I have written a letter to your grandson – a letter to teach him how to be a better dad than we were. And how good would that be?

For we are Indigenous fathers and we care for our children. We have loved, nurtured and provided for them; we've protected them and taught them how to survive and be proud of their culture. We have done as your father did, and his father, and so on, for generations that go back tens of thousands of years.

We were the first builders, craftsmen, storytellers, artists, fishermen, hunters, scientists, inventors, explorers, farmers, engineers, warriors, and healers. We were not conquerors of each other's lands. We did not strangle Mother Earth. We were her protectors. We are still all these things and so much more. We are a continuum of proud Aboriginal and Torres Strait Islander men – the fathers of the longest surviving culture on earth.

And now, Dad, as your hard exterior becomes brittle with age, I feel you. As dusk reaches your eyes – eyes that were too bright to look upon in my youth – I see you. I understand you, Dad. I love you.

I will always be your dear son,

Thomas

About the contributors

Stan Grant is a Wiradjuri, Kamilaroi and Dharrawal man, and also has Irish ancestry. He spent his childhood on the road, moving from town to town, living among his father's Wiradjuri family. It gave him an enduring cultural connection and a deep love of storytelling. Stan has been a journalist for more than three decades, most of that time working as a foreign correspondent in Europe, Africa, the Middle East and Asia. He spent over a decade living in and covering China, and reported the wars of Iraq and Afghanistan and conflicts from Pakistan to North Africa and South-East Asia. He is a three-time winner of the prestigious Australian Walkley Award. Stan has published numerous critically acclaimed, bestselling books, and wrote the internationally successful documentary The Australian Dream, focusing on the racism directed at AFL star Adam Goodes. He is currently International Affairs Analyst at the ABC and Chair of Indigenous/Australian belonging at Charles Sturt University.

Troy Cassar-Daley has released eleven studio albums throughout his thirty years of making music. A proud Gumbaynggirr/Bundjalung man, Troy's natural authenticity is the bloodline of his music that endears him to his ever-growing number of fans from every walk of life. Troy has been awarded numerous accolades, including thirty-seven Golden Guitars, four ARIAs, three APRA Song of the Year awards, nine Deadlys (Australian Indigenous Artist Awards), four CMAA Entertainer of the Year awards, plus two NIMAs (National Indigenous Music Awards). In 2017, Troy was honoured as the 50th inductee into the prestigious Australasian Roll of Renown. Throughout his life, Troy has shared his love of music with his father, his mother and his maternal uncles, and with his wife, Laurel, and their children Clay and Jem.

Yessie Mosby is a Zenadth Kes (Torres Strait Islander) Masig Island man, living in the Kulkalgal tribe area in the central Torres Strait Islands. He is a Traditional Owner, a father, an artist and craftsman. Yessie is a leader of the 'Our Islands Our Home' campaign to save his home from climate change inaction. As part of the campaign, eight Torres Strait Islanders from across Zenadth Kes have made a human rights complaint to the United Nations over climate change. They are known as the #TorresStrait8. Yessie is also the Torres Strait organiser with 350.org Australia, a not-for-profit organisation established to stand up to the fossil-fuel industry, and to support a just transition from coal, oil and gas to a renewable-energy future for all. The #TorresStrait8 complaint is an unprecedented action against a government about climate change inaction.

Charlie King has been engaged in community development, juvenile justice and child protection for decades. A youth worker for more than twenty years, he was also the chairperson of many boards, including the Northern Territory Department of Children and Families' Advisory Council, IMAC (Indigenous Men's Advisory Council) and the Bonner Committee (ABC Indigenous Advisory Committee). Charlie has been a sports commentator on the ABC since 1990, hosting *Grandstand*. He was the first Indigenous Australian to commentate at an Olympic Games, in Beijing 2008. Charlie has been working in partnership with CatholicCare NT since 2006, developing men's programs and the No More Campaign, targeting sporting codes to address violence in their clubs. His work has been recognised through a range of awards, including NAIDOC awards, Darwin City Council Citizen of the Year Award, Rotary awards and an Order of Australia Medal (OAM) for his services to the broadcast media and the Indigenous community. Most recently Charlie was awarded the Fitzgerald Social Change Award, and he is the 2019 Northern Territory Senior Australian of the Year.

Blak Douglas was born Adam Douglas Hill in 1970, in Blacktown, Western Sydney, to an Aboriginal father and a non-Aboriginal mother. Originally trained in illustration, photography and graphic design, observing a family of artisans, Blak became self-practiced in painting, with a style influenced by the study of graphic design and strongly politicised with a commitment to social justice. His works are collected by National Gallery of Australia, Art Gallery of NSW, National Maritime Museum, National Museum of Australia and regional council. A classically trained Yidaki (Didgeridoo) player, his performances include the Festival of the Dreaming, *Australian Idol* final, the Deadlys, Rugby World Cup Opening Ceremony, taking part in 'Requiem' by Peter Sculthorpe, and national and international tours with Musica Viva and Paul Jarman Projects.

Daniel Morrison lives in Perth, Western Australia. He has cultural connections to Noongar, Yamatji and Gija regions of Western Australia. He is engaged to his partner Jason and is a proud father of Mikayla and Daniel. Daniel has been Chief Executive Officer at Wungening Aboriginal Corporation since 2010. Wungening is a community-controlled Aboriginal organisation that provides culturally secure, confidential and free-of-charge services to Aboriginal people in communities around Perth in Western Australia.

Jack Latimore (Birpai-Thungutti) is a journalist and writer. He is the managing editor for NITV Digital and the executive producer and co-host of NITV's 'Take It Blak' podcast. He has previously worked for the *Guardian Australia*, *Koori Mail*, IndigenousX and the Centre for Advancing Journalism at the University of Melbourne. Jack has also been published by national and international outlets, including *Rolling Stone* magazine, GQ magazine, *Swampland* magazine, *Meanjin Quarterly*, *Griffith Review*, *Overland*, Black Inc. Books, UQP, Crikey, Z Net, the World Health Organisation, *Guardian Weekly*, Beat, Inside Story, and the ABC.

Joel Bayliss is a proud Wambaya and Gudanji man who has lived on Kaurna land his whole life. He is passionate about social justice. In response to a Bill Leak cartoon that portrayed a negative stereotype of Aboriginal fathers, Joel posted an image of himself and his two beautiful children, Ava and Isaiah, to Twitter. This single image led to a national movement known as #Indigenousdads, with thousands of images being shared – turning that negative stereotype into a positive one. Joel believes Reconciliation is the process where we as Australians acknowledge the past and move forward together, as Aboriginal and non-Aboriginal people.

Johnny Liddle is an Arrernte and Luritja man who grew up on Country in Central Australia, both on a station doing ringer's tasks as a boy, and in the bush learning traditional ways with his people. Johnny has worked many jobs, eventually finding his passion in Aboriginal men's health. He established Ingkintja Male Health, which provides services to Aboriginal men throughout Central Australia, and he was instrumental in facilitating the 2008 and 2010 Male Health summits. The summits were an important response to the way Aboriginal men were demonised by the 2007 Northern Territory Intervention. Johnny is a proud father and grandfather, who has always tried to pass on his knowledge to his sons.

Joe Williams is a Wiradjuri and Wolgalu man, born in Cowra, and raised in Wagga Wagga, New South Wales. Throughout a fifteen-year sporting career, Joe played in the NRL for South Sydney, Penrith and Canterbury, before switching to professional boxing. As a boxer, Joe was a two-time WBF World Jnr Welterweight champion and won the WBC Asia Continental Title. For most of his life, Joe battled severe mental illness. After a suicide attempt in 2012, he felt his purpose was to help people who struggle with mental health and wellbeing. Joe is an author, contributing to many books. His autobiography is titled *Defying the Enemy Within.*

Daniel James is an award-winning, Melbourne-based Yorta Yorta and Gunaikurnai writer and broadcaster. He hosts the 'Mission' on 3RRR FM and is the winner of the 2018 Horne Prize for his essay 'Ten More Days'. Born in Melbourne and raised on Taungurong Country in north-east Victoria, Daniel's work explores notions of empathy, intergenerational trauma, hidden history and the political landscape that continues to shape the lives of Aboriginal people across the country. He also examines what it means to be Aboriginal in the modern context, and the impact that political and societal attitudes continue to have on Aboriginal people, their sense of place and their sense of land.

Tim Sculthorpe is a proud palawa man from lutruwita (Tasmania). He is the founder of palawa kipli, the first Tasmanian Aboriginal food business, which saw Tim appear on ABC TV's *Further Back in Time for Dinner*. Tim's main focus today is as the Head of Marketing for Welcome to Country, a not-for-profit marketplace for Aboriginal and Torres Strait Islander products and tourism experiences. This work aligns with his life mission: to teach people about Aboriginal cultures for a more sustainable future. Tim hopes to reclaim that Australian Food is Aboriginal Food. Tim and his partner, Mariana de la Rosa, welcomed a son in 2019, their second best creation after the palawa kipli dish, the Bush Tuck-O.

Tristan Schultz is a Gamilaraay man of both Aboriginal and European Australian descendants. He has grown up on and lives on Yugambeh country in the Yugambeh language region of the wider Bundjalung Nation on the Gold Coast. Tristan is the Founder and Co-Director of Relative Creative, a Jellurgal (Burleigh Heads) Gold Coast strategic design agency that intersects strategic foresight and futures thinking, decolonial thinking, sustainable transitions, art and design. He has a Bachelor of Design, a Masters of Design Futures with Honours and a PhD in Design. Most importantly, he is a Dad to his daughter, Elke.

Tony Wilson is a Kaurna/Ngarrindjeri/ Narrunga artist based in Adelaide. He creates intricate and evocative artworks that explore themes of identity, collective resonance and connectedness. Heavily influenced by his cultural heritage, interactions with people and environment, Tony's work propels us to 'the space between our thoughts'. His work calls us to reconnect to our inner-selves while examining our relationships and the impact our interactions have on each other and our environment. Self-empowerment is a central theme in Tony's artistic practice, which is focused on visual arts that extends into local communities. He is passionate about sharing knowledge and connecting with young people through his work as an artist-in-residence in local schools, where he leads youth art mentoring programs. Tony's artistic work also includes digital art, graphic design and photography.

About the author

Thomas Mayo is a Torres Strait Islander man who lives on Larrakia Country in Darwin. A father of five children, he is a wharfie and union official for the Maritime Union of Australia. He has tirelessly advocated for the proposals in the Uluṟu Statement from the Heart, and is the author of two bestselling books. The first book, *Finding the Heart of the Nation: The journey of the Uluṟu Statement towards Voice, Treaty and Truth*, tells his story, the story of the Uluṟu Statement, and the stories of the remarkable people he met on his campaigning journey. A children's version, *Finding Our Heart*, was published in June 2020. At the same time as releasing this book, he has also released his latest children's book, *Freedom Day: Vincent Lingiari and the Wave Hill Walk-Off*, published by Bright Light.

Author acknowledgements

To the fathers and sons who contributed letters, thank you for your courage and determination to share our stories and our lessons, not just with our loved ones, but with the world. It was a pleasure and an honor to work with each of you.

To Tara June Winch, thank you for entrusting me with this idea, for your guidance and your generosity.

I thank Marcia Langton, Teela Reid, John Falzon, Olivia Williams, Jessica Hill, Ruby Langton-Batty and Yessie Mosby for your advice and guidance while I developed the concept and wrote my letter and poetry.

Thanks to the team at Hardie Grant, in particular Melissa Kayser and Astrid Browne; Bernadette for your brilliant editing and mentorship, Mike Kuszla for typesetting and Ella Woods for proofreading; and the deadly artist/illustrator, Tony Wilson, and designer, Tristan Schultz. Also the members and officials of the Maritime Union of Australia for always backing First Nations in our struggle for equality, fairness and justice.

Thank you to my children, Shayla, Tiah, Celestino, William and Ruby. Also my three eldest children's mum, Makezha Bin-Swani. You have all kept my letter writing true to the past, and grounded in the present.

Finally and most importantly, I thank my wife, Melanie Mayo, for your love, patience and understanding, and my mum, Elizabeth Mayo, for binding our families together with the greatest care in the world. I couldn't have written this without your support.

Published in 2021 by Hardie Grant Explore, an imprint of Hardie Grant Publishing.
Reprinted in 2026.

Hardie Grant Explore (Melbourne)
Wurundjeri Country
Level 11, 36 Wellington Street
Collingwood, Victoria 3066

Hardie Grant Explore (Sydney)
Gadigal Country
Level 7, 45 Jones Street
Ultimo, NSW 2007

hardiegrant.com/explore

Dictionary definition on p.83 retrieved from www.lexico.com/definition/colonization, April 2021

NATIONAL LIBRARY OF AUSTRALIA

A catalogue record for this book is available from the National Library of Australia

Hardie Grant acknowledges the Traditional Owners of the Country on which we work, the Wurundjeri people of the Kulin Nation and the Gadigal people of the Eora Nation, and recognises their continuing connection to the land, waters and culture. We pay our respects to their Elders past, present and emerging.

Dear Son
ISBN 9781741177565

10 9 8 7 6 5 4 3 2

Publisher: Melissa Kayser
Editor: Bernadette Foley
Proofreader: Ella Woods
Design: Tristan Schultz
Typesetting: Mike Kuszla

Colour reproduction by Splitting Image Colour Studio

Printed and bound in China by LEO Paper Products LTD.

FSC www.fsc.org MIX Paper | Supporting responsible forestry FSC® C020056

The paper this book is printed on is from FSC® certified forests and other controlled sources. FSC® promotes environmentally responsible, socially beneficial and economically viable management of the world's forests.